Rick Friedman *on*

Becoming *a* Trial Lawyer

# Rick Friedman

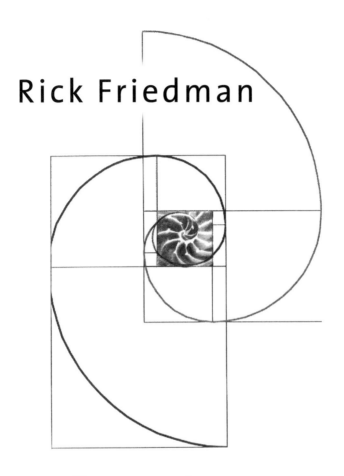

## *on* Becoming *a* Trial Lawyer

TRIAL
GUIDES

Trial Guides, LLC, Portland, Oregon, 97205
© 2008 by Rick Friedman.
All rights reserved. Published 2008.
Printed in the United States of America.

ISBN (cloth): 978–1–934833–04–9

Library of Congress Control Number: 2008907841

Trial Guides, LLC
Attn: Permissions
2400 SW Park Place
Portland, OR 97205
(800) 309-6845
www.trialguides.com

Trial Guides gratefully acknowledges the following people who have given their permission to have their works included in this volume:
Steven Pressfield, *Gates of Fire,* Bantam, 2005.
Mike Abourezk, assorted personal e-mail.

Illustrations by Jane Mayhook and Mindy Laymon.
Interior design by Laura Lind Design.
Cover design by Abraham Burns.

*To Kirsten,*

*My companion*

*from the fire-swamp*

*who still saves my life*

*every day.*

# Contents

# Publisher's Note

This book is intended for practicing attorneys. This book does not offer legal advice and does not take the place of consultation with an attorney with appropriate expertise and experience.

Attorneys are strongly cautioned to evaluate the information, ideas, and opinions set forth in this book in light of their own research, experience, and legal judgment, to consult applicable rules, regulations, procedures, cases, and statutes (including those issued after the publication date of this book), and to make independent decisions about whether and how to apply such information, ideas, and opinions to a particular case.

Quotations from cases, pleadings, discovery, and other sources are for illustrative purposes only and may not be suitable for use in litigation in any particular case.

All references to trademarks of third parties are strictly for informational purposes of commentary only. No sponsorship or endorsement by, or affiliation with, the trademark owners is claimed or implied by the author or publisher of this book.

The author and publisher disclaim any liability or responsibility for loss or damage resulting from the use of this book or the information, ideas, and opinions contained in this book.

# Acknowledgments

In my writing, as in many parts of my life, I rely heavily on the help and support of friends and family. Their work made this a much better book than I could have created myself. My thanks to Mike Abourezk, Jude Basile, Bill Cummings, Kim Dvorak, James Fitzgerald, Sharon Fitzgerald, Jackie Friedman, Kirsten Friedman, Stan Friedman, Gary Fye, Jim Gilmore, Jim Hertz, the ever patient Tina Ricks, and Ann Stockman.

Like all trial lawyers, I have benefited from the work of countless others who take the time to teach and write on the subject of trial advocacy. I hope this book expresses the best of what I have learned from these talented and generous lawyers. I am forever in their debt.

Thanks to Steven Pressfield for permission to quote from his excellent book *Gates of Fire*.

Finally, thanks to my friends in the Inner Circle—their wisdom has inspired me, their friendships have enriched and supported me.

# Introduction

If you are reading this, you are likely considering the prospect of becoming a trial lawyer. Maybe you have already embarked on that difficult journey. Maybe you are having second thoughts about the wisdom of your decision.

Becoming a trial lawyer is like traveling through a thick, dark, humid jungle. The strange and unfamiliar confronts you at every turn; progress often seems imperceptible; and yes, there are very real dangers.

There are excellent books on litigation tactics, trial technique, and even law office management. These can be helpful, but they concern themselves with the externals of being a trial lawyer. Ultimately, the journey toward becoming a trial lawyer—like all great journeys—is an inward one. You are changing from one thing—whoever you are—to another thing, a trial lawyer.

There are also excellent books, by extraordinary trial lawyers, recounting how they made their own way through the jungle. These too can be helpful; we can learn from the example set by others. But the path they took is their path, not yours. They started in a different place and will end in a different place.

What about *your* journey through the jungle? It is my hope that this book will serve as something of a guidebook for you. The path I took is long since overgrown. You will have to find your own, as everyone does. But if I can't tell you which path to take, perhaps I can teach you what quicksand looks like, direct you to some sweet fruit, and help you consider whether you want to make the journey at all.

This book is divided into three parts. Part I offers advice on how to get the knowledge and skill you need to be a trial lawyer. Part II identifies common errors made by trial lawyers everywhere, at all levels of experience. I chose these particular mistakes because the cause is often a psychological blind spot or misunderstanding, and the fix often seems counterintuitive and contrary to common lore and practice. I hope to not only save you the time, trouble, and heartache involved in repeating these particular mistakes, but more important, to demonstrate how crucial it is to observe clearly and think independently, whatever your level of experience or skill. Finally, Part III addresses the emotional and psychological challenges facing the trial lawyer. These challenges demand that we meet them with as much determination, passion, and humility as any other aspect of our calling.

Since this book is about you and your journey, I have tried to minimize the autobiographical. The focus should be on you. Still, you need to know three things about me in order to evaluate what I have to say.

The first thing you should know is that I am not a "natural" trial lawyer, as most people would commonly understand that term. Trying cases came harder for me than it does for most. When I began practicing law, I was socially awkward and painfully shy. The first time I stood in front of a jury panel and tried to ask questions in *voir dire,* my mouth opened, but no words came out. I tried to force air out of my chest and up into my throat to make sounds, but nothing happened. There was not a sound in the courtroom while my mouth opened and closed silently, like a goldfish's.

This was not the only attempt at making sounds. After doing my goldfish imitation for about thirty seconds, I went back to my table and purposefully rustled some papers around. I walked back in front of the jury and became a goldfish again. Back to the table for a drink of water (trying to hide my trembling hand) and once again to the center of the courtroom for everyone to see, unable to make a single sound.

Finally, the judge took mercy on me and gruffly said, "Well, if you're not going to ask them any questions, I will." That got the trial started.

This was not an isolated event. I had had equally humiliating experiences in moot court and in what passed for clinical education in law school. It was more than a decade before I could approach a jury with anything less than deep-seated dread. When my first felony trial began, I was five feet, eleven inches and weighed 160 pounds. The trial was over in five days, and I had lost 10 pounds. I had been unable to eat anything at all for the entire five days. Ten years later, defending in a criminal conspiracy trial, I would have breakfast and then go to the office and throw up—every weekday for five weeks. I tried to be quiet so my partner, Jeff Rubin, wouldn't hear. To this day, I don't know if he did.

The next thing you should know is that, as a trial lawyer, I am largely self-taught. I learned almost nothing about trying cases in law school. I left law school and began a solo practice in Sitka, Alaska. Sitka is on a three-hundred-square-mile island that can only be reached by boat or plane. At the time, Sitka's total population was about seven thousand, and the lawyer population was less than ten.

I had no mentor. I had to teach myself. That forced me to read everything I could about trials and trial lawyers. I watched trials whenever I could. Over and over I listened to audiotapes and watched videotapes of great trial lawyers like Racehorse Haynes and Moe Levine. I became a connoisseur of trial advocacy training materials—articles, books, audiotapes, videotapes. I bet few people in the country have consumed as much of this material as I have. Unfortunately, as discussed later in this book, much of it is boring, unhelpful, or worse (Levine and Hayes are among the exceptions). Finding the good stuff was a rare and joyous occasion.

I would take what I found in these books and tapes and try it out in the courtroom. I quickly had to learn the difference between good advice and bad. Over the years, I have tried all kinds of cases: drunk driving, first-degree murder, child custody, defamation, personal injury, commercial torts, products liability, and insurance bad faith. Like any self-taught practitioner, I have made just about every mistake you can imagine—and probably some that would never occur to you.

The last thing you should know is that I developed an unusual trial practice. Our firm is asked to try cases for other lawyers throughout the country. This provides the opportunity to see how law is practiced and cases are tried in a variety of locations. I have worked with, and against, some of the finest lawyers in the country. I have seen brilliant trial lawyers make mistakes and incompetents make some moves of pure genius.

While traveling around the country accumulating trial experiences, I've observed and learned from the people around me. In trying to find my way through the jungle, somewhere along the line I became a trial lawyer, but I never stopped asking what that means—and what it means for me as a person.

My hope for this book is that it can be a guide for those interested in becoming a particular kind of trial lawyer—the kind that represents people in court. I've spent a lot of time watching the other kind of trial lawyer, the kind who represents corporations and governments, but I have almost no experience navigating that jungle. If you want to enter there, this book will not be of much help.

My hope is that this book will comfort and ease your anxiety in some respects and goad you to action in others. I have tried to express my opinions and advice as directly and truthfully as I can.

# Introduction

I expect this book will annoy, even anger, many accomplished trial lawyers. They will note that they followed few, if any, of my suggestions. They will assume I am implying that if they didn't follow these suggestions, they must not be skilled trial lawyers. This is not my intent. I am describing a method of navigating through the jungle that has worked for me. It is not the only method.

I have not written a Bible or a rule book. I have not attempted to state a minimum "standard of care." Instead, I offer suggestions and standards for those who want to become the best trial lawyers they can be. Aspiring to these standards—even when I fell short—helped me become a better trial lawyer. I think they will help you too.

But what is true for me may not be true for you. My opinions may be wrong, and my advice misguided. There is no way to prove or disprove most of what I say except through your own personal experience. Take what seems helpful and discard the rest. It is *your* journey after all.

I have written the book I wish I had found when I started practicing law. If it can save you from some of the wounds I suffered or if it can help yours heal faster, I will consider it a success. Maybe it will even help us both find some peace in this least peaceful of professions.

*Rick Friedman*
*September 2008*
*Bremerton, Washington*

**Part I**

# *Entering the Jungle*

Do I have what it takes to be a trial lawyer? Why should I want to be a trial lawyer? What *is* a trial lawyer anyway?

In this first part of the book, I address these and other questions that seem to haunt all beginning trial lawyers. To say they haunt all beginning trial lawyers is misleading, though, because that implies they do not trouble more experienced lawyers. In fact, these questions follow us all throughout our careers. For the new lawyer, they can be a source of sharp, fresh pain; to the experienced lawyer, a dull familiar ache. How you adapt to the pain or anxiety these questions raise has much to do with the sort of person, and the sort of lawyer, you become.

A story is in order, because it makes it easier for me to present this book to you. It captures the spirit in which this book is offered. It may even bring you some comfort. It was the late 1980s. I had been practicing law for nine years. In Alaska, three first-degree murder acquittals occurred in the previous year, and one of them was my case. The defense lawyers in those three cases were asked to speak at the annual public defender conference. The conference organizers asked us to expound on the lessons we learned in achieving the acquittals.

The first lawyer to speak was one of the most brilliant trial lawyers I have ever met. When he stands before you, you know you are in the presence of greatness. The next lawyer to speak was not only extremely smart, but also charming and charismatic. When he finished, it was time for the moderator to introduce me.

"Every year after these conferences," said the moderator, "people come up to me and say things like, 'I'll never be as brilliant as Jim. I'll never be as charming and charismatic as Phil.' Here, to show you that you don't need to be brilliant, charming, or charismatic to win a first-degree murder case, is Rick Friedman."

This is a true story. True, not only because it actually happened, but because the point is well-taken. The qualities of a good trial lawyer are not generally well understood. A certain level of intelligence is required, but genius is not. Charm and charisma are helpful, but not essential. Instead, an odd kind of courage is required: willingness to work hard and fail, willingness to look foolish, willingness to expose yourself and risk rejection, and finally, willingness to look deep into your own soul. The job forces all of this on you. If you are up to the challenge, you might be successful. If not, you won't be.

# CHAPTER ONE

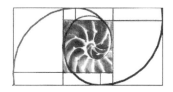

# Why Be a Trial Lawyer?

Why be a trial lawyer? This is worth asking at all points in your career. It's never too late to become a trial lawyer, and it's never too late to stop. You may never come up with a satisfactory answer, but the self-examination that comes from asking the question is important to your development as a trial lawyer and as a person. At a minimum, asking the question will remind you that you have a choice. No one is forcing this occupation on you. So, what are you trying to get out of it?

The traditional, socially acceptable answers are variations on such themes as helping others, fighting for what is right, combating the abuse of power, and the ever popular "wanting to make a difference." Each of these themes can help give meaning to your work as a trial lawyer. But any honest exploration of the reason for being a trial lawyer requires deeper inquiry.

The first thing to recognize is that the answer is a moving target, in the same way you are a moving target. Helping others or wanting to make a difference might attract you to trial work in college or law school, when career choices are somewhat abstract and hypothetical. But those same reasons might not be enough to sustain you at age thirty-eight, when you are working seventy-hour weeks, have two kids who need braces, and are having trouble making payroll.

Plenty of careers provide the opportunity to help others or make a difference. Most are not as all-consuming as trial work. Why be a trial lawyer? As you grow and change over time, the question requires that you constantly update the answer.

## What Is a Trial Lawyer?

For purposes of this book, I define a trial lawyer as someone who:

- Represents individuals (or small businesses) in litigation.
- Is committed to developing the ability to skillfully represent his or her clients in trials before judges and juries.
- Is committed to doing his or her best job in every single trial.

Notice there is no quantitative aspect to this definition. I would not claim you need a certain number of trials under your belt to call yourself a trial lawyer. Bush pilots in Alaska talk about how there are pilots with a thousand hours of experience and then there are pilots with one hour of experience repeated a thousand times.

The same is true of trial lawyers. There are some who have tried many cases, but would not fit my definition of trial lawyer. On the other hand, there are lawyers going into their first trial who would. One of the major goals of this book is to examine the sort of commitment this definition requires—the commitment this job requires.

## It Is a Hard Job

In any particular case, you will almost always be outmanned and outgunned. Although the psychological thrill of being the underdog can be substantial, the day-to-day reality is that you are constantly stretched to your limits. The primary way to make up for this disparity of resources is through your own extraordinary effort. Simply put, to even have a chance, you have to outwork your opponents— and they work hard.

In any individual case, there is almost always more work to do: another issue to research, another witness to interview, or another line of cross-examination to construct. Many of your cases alone could be full-time jobs. But you can't afford to make any one case a full-time job. So you find yourself cutting corners or making what you hope are prudent judgment calls. When you sleep late on Sunday or go to your child's school play in the middle of a work day, are you shortchanging your client?

Let's say you are a trial lawyer with twenty cases. That means a minimum of twenty smart, well-educated, well-financed, hardworking people are spending significant portions of their time and energy trying to figure out how to beat you. While you are at the movies Friday night, one of them is drafting a set of discovery to send you on Monday. While you are sleeping late Sunday morning, one of them is drafting a summary judgment brief. In criminal cases, an entire law enforcement agency may be interviewing witnesses while you are on vacation.

In response to this pressure, many trial lawyers work constantly. They work themselves into physical illness or mental or emotional dysfunction.

Then too, as trial lawyers we must work with the people who populate the litigation landscape: disagreeable judges, disagreeable defense counsel or prosecutors, and yes, on occasion, disagreeable clients. Sometimes we even have to deal with disagreeable partners or disagreeable co-counsel. Everyone waits and watches for us to make a mistake.

Whether we represent the accused in a criminal case or a plaintiff in a civil case, the jury—and most judges—view us with suspicion. We start in a hole before the case, the hearing, or the trial even begins. Because of this, mediocre prosecutors or civil defense lawyers can win most of their cases. A mediocre plaintiff's lawyer or criminal defense lawyer will win almost none.

Whatever your capacity for work, suffering, or sacrifice, this job demands it all. Whatever you give, you will always feel as though you are not giving enough. Why would anyone voluntarily jump into this stress-pool?

## Other Types of Lawyers Do Important Work

Plenty of interesting, challenging legal jobs contribute to the good of society. General practitioners help people daily—and often expose and correct governmental or corporate misconduct in the process. Class-action lawyers can help more people in a single well-executed case than a trial lawyer can help in a lifetime. Writers and researchers at plaintiff or criminal defense firms contribute every bit as much to the result as the trial lawyers who get the credit. So why be a trial lawyer?

## What About the Money?

Some superstar trial lawyers become enormously wealthy. Some lucky trial lawyers also become wealthy. The prospect of big money no doubt keeps many trial lawyers in the business. But being a trial lawyer is not a reliable way to become rich. The studies I have seen and the trial lawyers I have known suggest most trial lawyers make a good, but not a great living. If they put the same creativity, time, and energy into selling real estate or cars, they would probably make more money—and make it sooner.

Being a trial lawyer involves huge risk. For every trial lawyer who makes it rich, a hundred live on the brink of financial disaster, and scores go over the edge. The old adage has some truth: "Trial lawyers live rich and die poor." Many die poor. Most do not live rich. So why be a trial lawyer?

## Why Be a Trial Lawyer?

The reason for being a trial lawyer varies from person to person. It also differs from time to time in any person's life. Here are a few things to think about now. But as you will see, this entire book is my attempt to answer this question—for me and for you.

Some trial lawyers will answer that they like the variety—one day you're interviewing a Hell's Angel, the next you're interviewing a prize-winning physicist. No two days are ever the same. Others will tell you they like the freedom—you answer only to your conscience, your client, and your God. Gerry Spence gave a different answer—one that expresses a major theme of this book.

Spence has been my professional hero since I first heard about him in 1980. I read all his books, watched every continuing legal education (CLE) video of him I could get my hands on, and tracked down transcripts of his trials to read.

I got my first chance to meet Spence in the mid-1990s, when I received a call from one of his partners. They had a case in Alaska. Would I act as local counsel? They would do all the work; I just needed to make sure things were filed properly. What percentage would I charge?

I've never liked local counsel arrangements in which I did nothing but file pleadings prepared by someone else. It had been years since I'd agreed to one. But I saw my chance. I would do it for no fee, if the partner could arrange for me to have dinner with Gerry Spence. The partner quickly and incredulously agreed.

Spence had just finished the Randy Weaver defense in Idaho when we had our first meeting. This was the most recent in a long line of impossible cases he had won. We sat in a fancy restaurant in Anchorage, and I had the chance to ask him all the questions that had built up over the years. He was kind enough to try to give me his best answers. Finally, I worked up the courage to ask him what I most wanted to know. He had achieved more than anyone could hope to in the practice of law. He had trial victories, published books, financial success, and the adoration of tens of thousands of young lawyers. He was pushing seventy. Given the mental, physical, and emotional strain of trial practice, why was he still doing it?

He didn't need time to search for an answer. "It's the best way I've found to learn about myself."

As is often the case when I hear Spence's advice, I wasn't ready to hear this. It sounded too pat and a little narcissistic. But in the years that followed, I've come to realize he was absolutely right.

I originally thought of trial work as applied political science. The courtroom is where the rules of society are enforced. After a short time practicing, it became obvious that trial work is also applied psychology. I observed basic psychological principles at play in the conduct of the judge, the jury, the witnesses, the opponent, and myself—all constantly interacting. After a few more years of trial work, I could see applied philosophy at work in the courtroom. What is truth? What is justice? What can we really know about a subject? What is fair, what is moral, and what deserves punishment or reward?

All of this is part of what makes trial work so interesting and rewarding. Spence was right, however. There is more to it. Trial work can also be an inward journey. Seen in this light, trial lawyering is also applied spirituality. (There's a word you don't see in legal books very often.) By spirituality, I mean the process of turning inward to find truths about ourselves and about the world, truths that can sustain us and carry us beyond ourselves.

You can hide from yourself in any job. You can sleepwalk through life, trying to stay comfortable and secure. Certainly, some trial lawyers do that. But trial work makes that approach to life very difficult. Over and over, you come face-to-face with the sadness, unfairness, and injustice of the world. Over and over, you come face-to-face with your own character, weaknesses, and foibles.

As a trial lawyer, you exist in a crucible that will reveal truths about you and the world—whether you want to see them or not. Those who don't want to see them turn to alcohol, compulsive work habits, or various forms of narcissism. Or they cripple and blind themselves with their own cynicism. Or they find other ways to give up.

If you can resist these temptations to flinch and keep trying to become a trial lawyer, the process can be transforming. You might discover strength, maturity, courage, and compassion—in yourself and in others—that you didn't know existed. That may be the best reason to be a trial lawyer.

# CHAPTER TWO

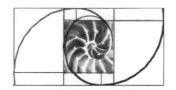

# Individual Billing Unit
# or Trial Lawyer?

D o law professors talk about widgets anymore? When I was in law school, they always talked about widgets. In Contracts class, we dealt with situations in which *A* promised to deliver twenty thousand widgets to *B* by July 15, but didn't deliver until July 20. In Torts class, widgets were destroyed by fire, flood, or auto accident.

My dictionary from that era defines *widget* as "a small mechanical device, such as a knob, switch, etc., especially one whose name is not known or cannot be recalled."[1] My professors emphasized a more important aspect of the widget—it was *fungible*.

If you are a law student about to enter the workforce, you are a widget. You won't be called this to your face, of course, although some firms might think of you as an IBU—individual billing unit. Your help makes the business run. You do legal research, write briefs, and take depositions. You are a mechanical device that helps the larger machine, the law practice, run smoothly.

Trials interrupt the smooth, predictable operation of just about any organization. Exceptions exist, of course, including many public defender and prosecution offices and some private law firms. But

---

1. *The Random House Dictionary of the English Language* (College Edition, 1968).

even in these, management's first interest is not developing your trial skills, but operating the organization smoothly and efficiently.

No matter how kind your employer, no matter how much your boss likes you, no matter what your superiors say about their commitment to developing your trial skills, to them you are mostly—well, a widget. To get opportunities to develop your trial skills, you will have to fight for them.

All the forces of the legal world push you away from trying cases. These include your bosses, your judges, and your financial self-interest, to name a few. Developing trial skills is the path of most resistance.

All trial lawyers are self-educated and self-made. You'll need help along the way, and with luck you may even find a mentor. But in the end, you have to take charge of your own education and development. No one can do it for you. You'll be a widget until you make yourself something else.

# CHAPTER THREE

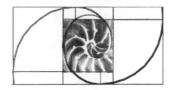

# Educating Yourself

How do you get from law-school graduation to comfort and skill in the courtroom? Here is the first hard truth: *Training yourself to become a trial lawyer is completely your own responsibility.*

Most law schools and employers make little effort to train students or young lawyers how to be trial lawyers. Even if you are lucky enough to land a job with an employer interested in developing your skills as a trial lawyer, the most your boss can do is provide opportunities and some guidance. Learning and growth are up to you.

Since becoming a trial lawyer is *your* goal, it's *your* responsibility. You decide how hard you want to work at it, how hard to push yourself. You learn your strengths and weaknesses and what you are going to do about them.

## Getting Trial Experience

The most common complaint of aspiring trial lawyers is the dearth of opportunities for trial experience. What they really mean—without knowing it, I believe—is that there are few opportunities to gain trial experience *at little or no cost.* Here is the next hard truth: *Money is the biggest obstacle to gaining trial experience.*

You could almost say money is the *only* obstacle to gaining trial experience. At every point in your career you will have opportunities for trial experience; almost always, money will be the most compelling (if unacknowledged) reason for not taking the opportunity. Let me illustrate my point with a few examples:

- Fresh out of law school, you might consider a job with a prosecutor's or public defender's office. These jobs will give you trial experience, but probably pay less than you would earn in private practice—where you would get little or no trial experience.

- In private practice with a big firm, you can take advantage of some of the trial opportunities discussed in this chapter, but only at the expense of reducing your billable hours. This will directly or indirectly cost you money.

- In solo practice, you can take court-appointed criminal work that will almost guarantee some trials—at $35 per hour. Or you can spend the same time drafting contracts and wills earning $125 per hour.

- In a personal injury practice, the economic incentives almost always favor settling a case rather than trying it. For example, imagine a case that should settle for $20,000. The maximum offer is $10,000. It will take you 100 more hours to prepare and try the case. If you value your time at $150 per hour and have a one-third contingency fee, you are economically better off accepting the $10,000 and not going to trial to win a $30,000 verdict. (Do the math.) And this is before you even factor in the risk of losing.

- In private criminal defense practice, you can structure fee agreements in various ways. Except with extremely wealthy clients, most of these structures result in a financial incentive to avoid trial.

As we review ways to obtain trial experience, you will notice a common thread—they are all contrary to your short-term monetary self-interest. With student loans to pay off, a family to support, or an office to maintain, the financial pressure to avoid trials is enormous. There is no way around this uncomfortable fact of life. So the question is, how much are you willing to pay for trial experience?

## Join a Prosecutor's or Public Defender's Office

Many prosecutor's and public defender's offices have good training programs. Others have training programs that consist of little more than handing you the evidence code and pointing you toward the courtroom. In either event, you won't find more opportunities to try cases than in a prosecutor's or public defender's office. Even if you ultimately want to do civil work, there is no better place to get started. You learn to deal with witnesses, judges, and juries. You learn the rules of evidence. You learn that life is not as simple, fair, or predictable as it appears on television.

I promised to warn you of the potholes and quicksand along the journey to becoming a trial lawyer. Let's talk about some of the most common obstacles facing lawyers who begin their careers at prosecutor's or public defender's agencies.

- **HEAVY CASELOADS CAN BREED BAD TRIAL LAWYER HABITS.** It's easy to use the caseload as an excuse to avoid the things you must face to develop as a trial lawyer. There's no time to read the state supreme court slip opinions, interview that potentially important witness, or write a better brief. At least that's what you tell yourself. Becoming a sloppy lawyer isn't your goal, but it can happen.

- **YOU GET COMFORTABLE AND LAZY.** You learn the job; you know the judges and clerks. The tempo of the courthouse becomes a natural,

personal biorhythm. The work becomes a job, not an adventure—
and not your own personal journey. You become a sloppy lawyer.

- **You become burned out and cynical.** You are confronted, hour
  after hour, with the cruelty and unfairness of the world. It is a lot
  to bear. You develop a cynicism that you think will protect you. It
  doesn't. But you stop growing and developing as a trial lawyer.

- **In criminal practice, deadlines are shorter, the practice is
  faster-paced, and mediocre briefs are more common.** Working
  in this environment can make it difficult to improve your own
  writing, both because less is expected of you, and because you
  are less likely to encounter good writing.[2]

- **Prosecutors get too used to winning.** Perhaps a more accurate way to say this is that they become too used to walking into
  court with the judge and jury predisposed in their favor. If you
  are always swimming with the current, you have less incentive
  to push yourself.

- **Most public defenders are going to lose a large percentage
  of their trials.** Losses early in a career cause many an aspiring
  trial lawyer to lose spirit or self-confidence. It can also cause the
  cynicism or laziness described above.

Despite these dangers, if I were to recommend an ideal career
path for aspiring trial lawyers, it would include two to three years
in a prosecutor's office followed by two to three years in a public defender's office. Young prosecutors learn to build and present a case. Public defenders learn how to break down a case and,

---

2. I cannot let this sentence stand without noting that some of the best legal writers I know
are criminal lawyers. They recognize how important motion practice is to trial outcome and
do what is necessary to keep their writing sharp, focused, and powerful.

more important, how to represent a living human being. After stints in each office, you will be that rare and marketable commodity: a young lawyer with extensive and varied trial experience. You can stay in criminal law or move into civil practice. You should have no trouble getting a well-paying job at a top-notch private litigation firm. Either way, the problem of advancing your own education as a trial lawyer remains.

## Watch Trials

Go to the courthouse and watch a trial from beginning to end. Many lawyers, even those who call themselves "litigators," have never done this. Watch the whole thing, jury selection to verdict. Then watch another and another. This counts. It is trial experience. You will learn important things.

Are you bored? The jurors probably are too. What could the lawyers do to avoid this? What are the lawyers doing well? What are they doing poorly? You are gaining experience. When it's time for your first *voir dire,* you will know the procedure in your jurisdiction.

Are there certain trial lawyers you admire? Make a point of watching them in trial—beginning to end. If you can only drop in on portions of a trial, that is better than nothing, but you can lose context that way. You lose the feel of the trial. Part of what you are trying to cultivate is your own sense of how things feel in the courtroom.

You will learn some things more quickly this way (such as how not to bore the jury) than by actually trying a case. Without concern about your own performance or the result, you can observe dispassionately and objectively.

So what are we talking about here? A week away from work? Maybe two or three? This is expensive. It's also a valuable and worthwhile experience. How badly do you want to be a trial lawyer?

## Volunteer to Work for Free

If you are going to be watching a trial anyway, why not volunteer to help? Approach a trial lawyer you respect and offer to work for free. Tell him you would like to donate twenty hours of your time before the trial on any aspect of the case related to the trial. During the trial day you would like to sit in the courtroom (in the back or at counsel's table), and after hours you will help any way you can.

## Court Appointments

Check with the municipal, state, and federal public defender's agencies in your area. Many have programs that hire private counsel for cases in which the agency has conflicts. Sometimes the local court system administers these programs, so check there too. If you have little to no experience, tell them, but express your willingness to handle even the smallest case if it will get you into court.

## Take Cases to Trial

For a civil attorney, there is always economic pressure to settle every case. If you push back strongly against this pressure, you will try more cases.

Your client's interests must come first, but it can be difficult to discern where the client's interests lie.[3] In a low-offer soft-tissue injury case, the client may gain next to nothing by accepting the offer. The client has nothing to lose by going to trial. Lawyers tend to settle these cases because they lose time and money by trying them—and they risk a damaged ego to boot. Over the years, insurance companies have tuned in to these dynamics, and their offers have become smaller and smaller.

---

3. This is a tricky issue, discussed more fully in Chapter 28.

Take a case in which you value the compensatory damages at $30,000. You have $2,000 of costs into the case, and the highest offer you get is $5,000. The client risks $2,000 by going to trial, but stands to recover approximately $18,000 if you get a fair verdict. Most clients would see going to trial as in their self-interest. Some lawyers work hard to convince clients otherwise—telling them about hard-nosed jurors and erratic judges.

There is no shortage of these cases. Most lawyers don't want them. But if you want trial experience, this is an excellent place to start.

## Do Pro Bono Work

As a private attorney, you will meet clients who need someone to go to court with them. They may not be able to pay. If the case will get you to trial, it may be worth taking, even if it doesn't pay in money. I know one fairly experienced trial lawyer who agreed to try a murder case for $3,000, because he badly wanted to handle a murder case. The money didn't even cover his expenses, but he got a murder case under his belt. He didn't slacken his effort because of the low fee, and an extraordinary learning experience was his reward.

## Practice Before Administrative Agencies

Numerous state and federal administrative agencies hold trial-like hearings on a regular basis. Develop an expertise in one of the areas handled by these agencies and go to hearings. Hearings are usually more informal than court trials, but require many of the same skills. One attorney I know practiced before public utilities commissions for years before she was able to get her first civil trial. When she did, it was a medical malpractice trial against some of the best defense lawyers in her state. She not only won, but got a stunning verdict. She had been a trial lawyer well before her first trial, honing her skills in every way she could.

## Bring in Co-counsel

If you don't want to work for free and want to try a case you're not yet qualified for, bring in co-counsel. Better to split the money and get the experience than to settle too cheaply. The process of preparing for trial with an experienced lawyer and then second-chairing a strong presentation will build your skills and confidence. It is also a way to establish strong friendships and build your practice.

## Conduct Your Own Focus Groups

For a focus group, bring together five to twelve people *you don't know.* You can find these people through church, by running an ad, or by asking friends and coworkers to ask their acquaintances. You will be surprised how many people will be intrigued enough to show up for $25 and all the pizza they can eat.

Give your focus group the most limited version of the facts that you can. "Mr. Smith is charged with assaulting Mr. Jones in a bar. Mr. Smith says it was self-defense." Or "Mrs. Johnson was hit in a crosswalk on Oak Street. She claims she has a mild brain injury and permanent back injuries and is asking for compensation. Mr. Matthews admits the accident was his fault, but says Mrs. Johnson is seeking too much compensation."

Then ask your group questions like:

- What do you think the law should be in a case like this?
- Why?
- What other facts would you want to know to decide this case?
- Why?

Don't push the group members into consensus or resolution. It is the give-and-take of ideas, the way the group debates, that you will learn from, not the result. Slowly feed the group more facts and notice how those facts affect people's reactions and arguments.

Plenty has been written about conducting focus groups. My point here is that a lawyer doesn't need professional help to get a group of people in a room and see how they react to a case. Mike Abourezk, an exceptional trial lawyer from South Dakota, says he often learns more from a focus group of this type than from ten trials. He makes an excellent point.

Using simple focus groups, you will become more comfortable talking to strangers about the facts of your case—something that must be done at trial. You can also get outside your own head and see your case from other perspectives. Arguments that would never occur to you are presented on a silver platter. But more important are the changes that occur inside you. I quote from an e-mail Mike Abourezk sent me on the subject, as he says it better than I could:

> *Doing these groups myself also profoundly changes my attitude toward the jurors, which is a very big deal. Instead of going into trial feeling like half of the jurors are conservative jerks, and are secretly out to get me and my client, I go in there feeling okay about them. Most importantly, I am confident that in the end we will like each other. I feel that way because that is invariably the experience I have with my focus groups, and it profoundly affects how I act when I meet the jury....*
>
> *I can't describe all the things that happen for me in doing these groups myself, because much of it I can't define. But it is one of the most important*

*things I have ever stumbled on. I think the main prob-
lem other people have in doing focus groups is that
they think they need to hire experts for outrageous
amounts of money in order to benefit, which is a
myth that some experts perpetuate. The real benefit is
the personal emotional/social experience, and it does
me no good to hire someone else to get that for me.*

As you search for focus-group jurors, make a special effort to find
conservative jurors. I mean jurors more likely to be hostile to your
case. Ask the pastor at a conservative church if you can rent a conference room and put up a bulletin to recruit participants. Use Rotary
Club or Chamber of Commerce newsletters. Remember, you're not
looking for people to echo your own viewpoints; you are looking
for people who think and feel differently. Then, they need to be allowed to express their thoughts and feelings without feeling that
you are trying to persuade them to adopt your point of view. All of
this will make you a better trial lawyer.

## Attend CLE Workshops

More and more legal education seminars have hands-on practice
components. The American Association for Justice (AAJ), the National
Institute for Trial Advocacy (NITA), and the National Association of
Criminal Defense Lawyers (NACDL) offer many excellent programs
of this type. They are worth trying, if only to get exposure to a variety of styles and techniques and for practice in applying trial techniques in public. A word of warning: some of the programs may be
rigid and dogmatic. Some of the instructors can be poor teachers (and
maybe mediocre lawyers). Even worse, the instructor might be a ter-
rific teacher and know little about trying cases. Just because some
criticize your performance at a CLE workshop does not mean they

know what they are talking about. It's *your* job to separate the wheat from the chaff. Pay sincere attention and try to learn what they have to teach. Later you can decide what to use and not use in court.

It's apparent from this list that all of these opportunities for trial experience will cost you money. They will also be inconvenient. The forces of your personal and professional life will push you away from them. You must be aggressive. This is *your* education and goals we are talking about. How much trial experience can you afford? How much money are you willing to give up to become a better trial lawyer? You need to ask these questions. You can get as much experience as you are willing to pay for, both in time and in money.

The next hard truth is this: *If you do all of these things to get experience, it is still not enough*. You must do more to train yourself to be a trial lawyer.

## Learn the Law

The law you learned in law school is not enough to sustain you in a trial career. It's a good start at best, a firm foundation.

What are the intricate legal issues and principles in your areas of practice? How do the legal principles interact and apply to create actual results? How is your state supreme court interpreting critical provisions of the evidence code? It is your job to learn.

In a way, learning the law better is the easiest part of becoming a trial lawyer. You went to law school; you must have some aptitude for reading and thinking about the law. Only now, it should be much more interesting. Now, what's at stake is not a grade, but winning or losing—in public. Winning or losing your client's freedom, your client's job, or your client's money.

Legal principles are your weapons. You would not go into battle without a gun—a gun you had meticulously cleaned and cared for.

Yet many lawyers go into court with little working knowledge or re-gard for the law. Just last year I heard a defense lawyer speak dis-missively of motion work saying, "That's what associates are for." It is no coincidence that he and his client suffered a serious defeat just a few months later—a defeat brought about in large measure when the other side outmaneuvered him on the law.

The most famous trial lawyers still write many critical briefs them-selves. Multimillionaire trial lawyers in their seventies can tell you about the latest cases in their jurisdictions and debate the fine points of the legal doctrines involved. That is part of the reason they are multimillionaires.

You are a lawyer representing people, yet many aspects of the system are stacked against you. You cannot afford to give away any advantage—and the law often provides you with significant advan-tages. But you won't know that unless you keep studying.

A good place to begin is by reading your state supreme court slip opinions. At first, read them *all,* even the family law and workers' com-pensation opinions. People will come to you with family law and work-ers' compensation questions, even if you don't handle such cases. Every lawyer needs at least rudimentary knowledge of these areas. The same is true of opinions in other areas. You will be surprised how often your career carries you into unfamiliar legal fields. In most states, it's of great benefit to read the court of appeals' opinions too, although it may not be practical in large states such as California.

Read each opinion with an eye toward learning something. What does the opinion tell you about its author? About a particular eviden-tiary or contract principle? After a few years, you may want to stop read-ing opinions dealing with areas of practice you never enter—criminal law or family law, for example. But keep reading the others, even when the cases seem unrelated to cases you are presently handling.

The law truly is a seamless web. Everything is connected to everything else. The interpretation of an evidence rule in a criminal case can be the holding that helps you exclude or admit a critical piece of evidence in your civil trial—even if you don't do criminal work. The converse is true for criminal lawyers.

Subscribe to *Lawyers USA* or the *National Law Journal*. Read the summary of cases each newspaper contains. You will get a sense of what is going on in other jurisdictions. Look for cases or legal principles that could help with your existing cases. I seldom make it through an issue without finding citations that might have bearing on a case I am handling. At least two or three times a year, I strike gold.

Become a member of AAJ, NACDL, or both, and read the monthly magazines closely. Some of the best lawyers in the country describe how they handle the same problems you face. The same goes for the American Bar Association (ABA); join the sections that most interest you and read their periodic journals.

If you follow my recommended reading program, over the years you will notice that many of the new holdings and principles in one specialized area of law migrate over time into others. Being aware of these trends is an advantage over opponents. This awareness makes you a more creative and innovative lawyer. The law will be your friend, not a tedious duty.

Where do you find the time for all this reading? Buses, subways, and airplanes are good places and work for me. Maybe before bed or while eating lunch alone in the office. It is a discipline. Find the time the way you would for anything that is important to you. Quickly the reading gets easier and faster and even becomes fun. You will begin to notice overlap. The case you read about in *U.S. Law Weekly* is the subject of an article in *Trial* magazine six months later. You can begin to skim.

This is a treasure hunt for weapons to help you win cases. And you are filling your mind with the law. When the judge throws you a question out of legal left field, you'll be ready.

## Learn Trial Techniques

Trial lawyers love to talk and write about trials. They particularly like to talk about the mechanics, the technical and performance aspects of trying cases. Trial lawyers swap trial techniques the way kids swap baseball cards or fishermen swap advice on bait, lures, and tackle. Unfortunately, like advice from fishermen, much trial technique advice is little more than superstition, hunch, or personal bias. On the other hand, some gifted lawyers have shared creative and brilliant techniques in books, articles, and tapes.

Reading books and articles, attending CLE workshops, and watching videos will expose you to more trial technique options than a busy lawyer could ever encounter in court during a lifetime of practicing law. That is why it is important to stay exposed to these sources on a regular basis.

The Recommended Reading List at the end of this book contains some of the best books in existence on trial techniques. Why not read every book on this list? It's a way to not only learn much in the way of technique, but also to more readily tell the difference between good trial advice and bad.

You need good judgment to become educated on trial techniques. Keep these thoughts in mind as you exercise that judgment:

■ **IF THERE APPEARS TO BE A CONSENSUS ABOUT A PARTICULAR TECHNIQUE, THIS DOES NOT MEAN IT IS A GOOD TECHNIQUE.** Or if it's a good technique, that doesn't mean it's right for you or your particular trial.

When I started practicing law, the universal consensus was that *voir dire* was where skillful lawyers did their best to argue their case to the jury. It seemed as though every book and article I read made this point and backed it with cogent arguments showing why this was the best approach. That view is now discredited, replaced by the belief that you should have two primary goals in *voir dire:* building rapport with the jurors and identifying the "bad" panelists, so you can get them off the jury.

■ **EVEN AN EXCELLENT SOURCE MAY IN ONE BREATH GIVE YOU BRILLIANT ADVICE AND IN THE NEXT GIVE TERRIBLE ADVICE.** A good example is the book *Cross-examination: Science and Techniques* by Larry S. Pozner and Roger J. Dodd. This is an inspired book—one of the best books on trial technique ever written. It breaks the components of a good cross-examination into easily digestible bites. By following the book's instructions, almost anyone can do a creditable job in any cross-examination, even with little or no experience.

No better book is available for learning cross-examination techniques. However, in emphasizing their points, the authors go on to make suggestions like, "Only ask leading questions," and "Never ask questions to which you do not know the answer." They become dogmatic and rigid about what a good cross-examination looks like. In the process, their readers are not well served. I am not writing a book on trial technique, so I won't go into this issue here, other than to note that Pozner and Dodd show you how to make and sharpen a beautiful sword and then tell you never to use any other weapon. Everything they say about the sword is true; the advice to never use anything else is misplaced. So read, but with a critical and discerning eye.

I showed an early version of this chapter to a young lawyer who followed up with this question: "How do you tell bad advice from good?"

I would suggest that you can divide most trial tactic advice into two categories: preparation advice and execution advice. For example, much of Pozner and Dodd's book describes how to accumulate and organize materials you will use in cross-examination. This is preparation advice. In *Rules of the Road,* Pat Malone and I suggest drafting your jury instructions early in the litigation, long before trial. Again, this is preparation advice. If advice is about preparation, I would say try it. You can never be too prepared. If, after a few tries, you think the work is not worth the effort, change your approach.

Execution advice is concerned with how to behave or do your job in the courtroom. When considering this advice, be aware there is no one formula or approach to bring you success in every case. One behavior or approach may work well in one case and be terrible in another. Take the common advice to not ask a question on cross-examination to which you don't know the answer. You *must* understand why the proponents of this view feel so strongly about it; you must understand why it is often good advice. But there are many cases in which good advocacy *requires* that you ask questions to which you don't know the answer. Always beware of advice that suggests there is only one right way to do your job in the courtroom.

When considering execution advice, think about how your family or friends would react to the approach you're considering. Would they respond positively or negatively? How does it feel to *you* to act this way?

The goal is to become educated in trial tactics the way you might learn philosophy or martial arts. You want to know the universe of ideas or techniques available, even if they won't all work for you. When you have a comprehensive idea of your choices, then it is a matter of using your judgment and choosing. You have a shovel, a hammer, and a pick. Which do you use? If you only understand how to use a hammer, you will keep using it, whether it is the appropriate tool or not.

■ **FINALLY, YOU WALK A FINE LINE WHEN EXPERIMENTING WITH TRIAL TECHNIQUES.** You should push yourself to try techniques that feel awkward or unnatural, but never use any technique that doesn't feel honest or authentic. This may seem contradictory, but it is not.

An example of a technique that caused me trouble for years is looking jurors in the eyes at various points during the direct or cross-examination of witnesses. I would watch some lawyers do this, and it seemed like an effective way to bond and communicate with the jury. I would watch others do this and be convinced they looked like phony grandstanders. When I tried to do it, it felt phony and forced. I'm sure my natural shyness contributed to this feeling. It also felt a little rude—as if I were intruding on the jurors' personal space. So I stopped trying.

Yet, time after time, when I would watch the most experienced, gifted trial lawyers, they would periodically make eye contact with the jury while conducting direct or cross-examination. So from time to time, I would try again. It took over twenty years of trying cases before I *began* to feel comfortable looking the jurors in the eyes while asking questions. I think it makes me a better trial lawyer.

Looking the jurors in the eyes at various points in examining a witness is honest and authentic to me—even though it did not come naturally—because I truly *wanted* a closer connection with the jurors. My shyness was getting in the way. If I had stuck with what felt comfortable, I would never have learned how to do this. By watching others do it well, I was able to convince myself it could be effective, not phony—and that gave me the courage to keep trying.

Learning most techniques involves a similar—though not necessarily as lengthy—process. First, you must become convinced that the technique is not a gimmick, but adds to legitimate communication in the courtroom. Then you must be willing to push yourself to risk looking foolish. If you are honestly trying to communicate the truths of your case, the jurors will forgive you for not flawlessly executing the technique. If, instead, you are trying something new because it looked compelling in a CLE seminar or you think it will dazzle the jurors, you will lose points with them; they may even punish you.

## Learn About People

Good trial lawyers try to know and understand people: how they act, what is important to them, what motivates them. Some people have a natural gift for understanding people; the rest of us have to work at it. But the world provides innumerable opportunities for study.

Part of becoming a trial lawyer is studying people, whenever the chance arises. *Listen* to the people in the checkout line. *Ask questions* of the person sitting next to you on the subway. *Develop your people skills.*

Do you look people in the eye when you talk to them? Do you listen to what they have to say—do you try to understand the world from their point of view? The skills for ordinary interactions are some of the same skills needed in the courtroom. This means you have opportunities to practice trial skills every day. When you view the world through a trial lawyer's eyes, every encounter is an opportunity to improve your abilities in the courtroom. The trick is to keep working to develop your trial lawyer's eye and ear.

Another opportunity to do this is in watching public performances—or more accurately—the audience's reactions to public performances. How do speakers get the crowd's attention? How do they keep it? How do they lose it? When Meryl Streep, Judi Dench, and Forrest Whittaker deliver their lines, what is it that makes them so effective? When Jimmy Stewart and Tom Hanks seem to stumble and trip all over themselves as they speak, why is that so effective?

## Watch How You Treat People

Treating people with respect and kindness is more than just good manners; it is an effective way to become a better trial lawyer—for three reasons.

First, how you treat people becomes a habit. If you treat your food servers, taxi drivers, and staff as servants, you are likely to have a high-handed or superior attitude toward witnesses and jurors. Lawyers who try to turn that attitude off in the courtroom usually come across as obsequious and arrogant—simultaneously.

Second, paying attention to how you treat people causes you to notice things you would otherwise miss. Being kind and respectful toward your food servers, taxi drivers, and staff requires that you see them as individual people with characteristics all their own rather cardboard cutouts playing roles. Your skills at understanding people will improve, and these are skills essential for an effective trial lawyer.

Third, paying attention to how you treat people forces you to pay attention to aspects of yourself that might otherwise escape your attention. What are the obstacles within you that stand in the way of treating this particular store clerk with kindness and respect? Do you tend be impatient? Self-important? Aloof? You carry these characteristics with you into the courtroom. You might as well explore them ahead of time.

## Conclusion

Becoming a trial lawyer is a lot of hard work. You are responsible for educating yourself in this occupation. You are responsible for *keeping* yourself educated. With this responsibility comes a great deal of freedom and power. You get to *choose* what to read, whom to watch, which trial opportunities to take, and which ones to pass by. There are no shortcuts and no easy paths. But the path you take will be uniquely your own.

# CHAPTER FOUR

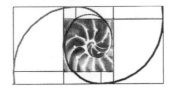

# Do You Have What It Takes?

*The second time I ever saw you I learned what I had read in books but I never had actually believed: that love and suffering are the same thing and that the value of love is the sum of what you have to pay for it and anytime you get it cheap you have cheated yourself.*

—CHARLOTTE, IN WILLIAM FAULKNER'S *The Wild Palms*

D̲o you have what it takes to be a trial lawyer? Most trial lawyers have asked themselves this question many times. I've been asking myself this question for almost thirty years. In my attempts at an answer, I closely studied good and bad trial lawyers, happy and miserable trial lawyers, experienced and inexperienced trial lawyers. In fact, I have studied just about every trial lawyer I have known.

You can learn a lot from watching other trial lawyers, but comparing yourself to others won't tell you if you have what it takes. The problem is that comparison supports whatever mood you are in at the moment. You might think, "She's so much smarter than I am. I could never be that good," or, "He's got an obnoxious personality. I could kick his butt in any trial."

To figure out if you have what it takes to be a trial lawyer, I suggest looking inward, not outward. To look inward, first clear away three pernicious myths about trial lawyers that can get in the way of a fair evaluation.

## Myth #1: The Star System—It's a Question of Talent

The thrust of the first myth is that either you are one of the fortunate few to have been born with the talent for trying cases—or you are not. You can often find the fortunate few speaking at CLE seminars and displaying their God-given talent for all to see. In subtle and not so subtle ways, they often communicate, "I am here to teach, but what accounts for my success can't be taught."

In fact, many successful trial lawyers initially showed little or no talent for trying cases. Perhaps the most notable is Gerry Spence, who by his own account failed the Wyoming bar exam. After passing it on the second try, he proceeded to lose his first eight trials.

Over the last fifty years, Spence has had one of the most spectacular careers of any trial lawyer in American history. In hindsight, it is easy to claim he was born with an exceptional talent for trying cases. Early in his career, however, no one—including Spence—would have suspected that. If "talent" implies that trying cases came easy for him, then nothing could be farther from the truth. Again, by his own account, he was an awkward, difficult personality, not at all comfortable in the courtroom. Throughout his career, even at the height of his success, he worked harder to develop trial skills than any lawyer I have heard of.

Granted, you need some combination of intelligence, people skills, and emotional resilience to become a good trial lawyer. But more people have these qualities in sufficient quantities than the star system and its proponents would suggest.

It has even occurred to me that there might be an inverse relationship between how easy trying cases comes and how good at it someone actually becomes. Jake Ehrlich was an enormously successful criminal lawyer in Los Angeles in the mid-twentieth century. Through sheer brilliance, he won one impossible case after another. Only his closest friends and family knew that whenever he went to trial, he broke out in hives all over his body. Despite all sorts of prescriptions and medications, the hives would not go away until the day after the verdict was rendered.

Most of the supremely successful trial lawyers I know pay a huge personal price for going to trial. This is because, despite their brilliance or talent, trying cases doesn't come easily to them—it is hard. Trial lawyers are made—self-made—not born.

## Myth #2: Anyone Can Be a Trial Lawyer

In a sense, the second myth is true. Anyone with a bar card can go into court and represent clients. On the other hand, not everyone is suited for the job. Extreme proponents of this myth would say trying cases can be taught—just like accounting. You learn the tried and true principles, you practice these principles, and then you apply them.

In fact, trying cases is part science, part craft, and part art. If you are not willing to study the science, practice the craft, and live the art of trying cases, you are doomed to mediocrity. Similarly, flawlessly applying the principles alone will not get you very far. This is *not* accounting.

Some people simply don't have the qualities required for success as a trial lawyer. That is a fact. Maybe they are not smart enough or don't have the people skills. Maybe they lack emotional resilience. Not everyone *can* be a trial lawyer. Just don't be too quick to judge yourself harshly.

The smarter lawyer or the lawyer with superior people skills often loses. This can be frustrating if you are that lawyer. It should also give us all hope. You can win without being the smartest or the most charming person in the room. (I have done it many times.) We all have a chance. However, if you don't have extraordinary emotional resilience, you are in trouble.

Much of this book is aimed at helping you deal with the emotional beatings trial law inflicts upon you. For now, it's enough to say that if you can't take regular doses of frustration, unfairness, sadness, grief, anger, and difficulty—and continue to enjoy life—you will not be able to consistently try cases over the long term. Emotional resilience is an absolute job requirement.

## Myth #3: Everyone Should Want to Be a Trial Lawyer

Fewer and fewer cases go to trial. We are moving—especially in civil cases and in urban areas—to a *de facto* solicitor/barrister system. Running an active litigation practice while being in trial enough to develop and maintain trial skills is becoming more and more difficult. One important consequence is that lawyers who rarely, if ever, first-chair a jury trial do much of the good in the justice system.

These lawyers are the unsung heroes of the trial bar. They sit at their desks and come up with the legal theories that make governments and powerful corporations legally accountable. They tenaciously pull damning documents out of corporate cellars for all to see. They withstand barrage after barrage of motions in order to get justice for their clients.

A TV show about a courageous litigator winning motions to compel production of documents will probably never hit the airwaves. But if we limited our vocational choices to what we see on TV, we would all be trial lawyers, ER doctors, and advisers who make over houses, cars, and people for a living.

It seems to me the most important questions you should ask are, "Who am I?" and "What is the job that gives me the best opportunity to express who I am?"

With these thoughts in mind, here are some things I think I know about what it takes to be a trial lawyer.

## There Are Many Kinds of Trial Lawyers

Although rare individuals are good at trying any kind of case from any side of the courtroom, most of us find we are more suited to one role or another. This is a function of skill, personality, interests, and temperament. On a primal level, it may have much to do with our attitude toward power and authority.

If you identify more with power and authority, you will probably be more comfortable as a prosecutor or a civil defense lawyer. If you like to push back against power and authority, you will probably be more comfortable as a criminal defense or civil plaintiff's lawyer. Yes, I know. This is gross oversimplification. But look around. It's mostly true.

Maybe you've been trying plaintiffs' cases and just can't get excited about trying to get money for a broken arm. Maybe you've been defending civil cases and can't get excited about using your ability and resources to pummel widows, orphans, and the handicapped. Consider what you are doing, and see if your heart is in it. If it isn't, it will show.

It is very possible you have what it takes to be a prosecutor, but not a criminal defense lawyer. If you think you are in the wrong trial role, talk to someone trying the type of cases you might want to try. Trial lawyers come in many varieties. Some try only employment cases (representing either employers or employees), some try only criminal misdemeanor cases, some try only construction cases. You may need to try many types of cases before you find where you belong.

It is also true that many trial lawyers enjoy trying a wide variety of cases. Take a good honest look at yourself. Then take a good honest *feel* of yourself. Where does it feel as though you should be going—even if that doesn't make logical sense? Too many lawyers have *thought* themselves into the wrong job. Trust your instincts; they are probably more reliable than your conscious brain. Most successful people have felt their way along, groping in the dark through much of their careers. Some types of cases will be easier or more exciting or more satisfying for you. Pay attention to how things feel, and you will ultimately end up in the right place.

Of course, "the right place" is constantly changing. How many criminal defense lawyers over the age of fifty are still trying cases? By that age, most move on to less harrowing jobs.

## No Particular Personality Type Is Necessary

Over the last ten years, I have had the privilege to meet some of the top trial lawyers in the country. Their names are familiar to anyone who does trial work. They have won huge verdicts, obtained impossible acquittals, written books, and been featured on television and in the movies. In regard to personality, guess what they all have in common? *Nothing,* other than a willingness to work extremely hard. Some are handsome, gifted athletes; some are awkward nerds. Some come from the poorest of backgrounds; others, from the ranks of the privileged. Some are painfully shy; others, charming and gregarious.

One other thing these lawyers share is that they didn't let their perceptions of their own shortcomings stop them from trying cases.

## It's Never Too Late to Start or Stop

One of the best trial lawyers I ever knew did not even finish law school until his mid-thirties. Another excellent trial lawyer I know tried her first case at age forty. Generally speaking, added years mean reduced stamina, but also increased confidence, character, and gravitas. If you want to be a trial lawyer, your years should not deter you.

On the other hand, I know lawyers who tried cases for twenty years before concluding that it was not for them. Your idea of who you wanted to be at age twenty should not dictate how you live your life at forty. If you don't enjoy your life as a trial lawyer, why not get out?

## Track Records Don't Mean Much

Some types of cases are harder than others to try. If you've been defending criminal cases and winning 30 percent of the time, those are good results. If you are prosecuting criminal cases or defending medical malpractice cases and winning 80 percent of the time, those are poor results. These days, if you are representing plaintiffs in minor injury cases and winning more than 30 percent of the time, consider yourself a trial genius.

Trials are not like baseball. The stats don't provide an objective basis for evaluation. Don't be too hard on yourself by comparing your record defending criminal cases with the record of your friend defending small personal injury cases. Don't give yourself a false sense of confidence by doing the reverse.

Every time I win a trial, a small voice in my head says, "You had good facts. Anyone could have won that case." When I lose, the voice says, "Ray Brown would have won that case. Don Keenan would have won that case." The voice goes on and on.

I hope for your sake you don't have an inner voice like mine, but you do need a way to understand your wins and losses. Why did you win? Why did you lose? What could you have done differently to improve the presentation or to improve the result?

The most meaningful measurement may be your track record with respect to your opponents' offers. If you regularly beat your opponents' offers, you are probably doing a good job. If you can't seem to beat those offers, you are either performing poorly in the courtroom, or you are a poor judge of case value. Your skills in both areas need improvement.

## You Have to Be Willing to Work Hard

I don't know a single successful trial lawyer who doesn't work like a dog. In fact, I don't know many *marginally* successful trial lawyers who don't work like dogs. Hard labor simply has no substitute. This point was highlighted a while ago as I listened to the tape of Harvard professor Larry Tribe arguing before the Indiana Supreme Court.

Tribe may be the foremost constitutional scholar in the last hundred years—maybe longer. He is also one of the most successful appellate advocates of the last hundred years. By Tribe's standards, his case in Indiana was a small one.

As I listened to the argument, it was quickly apparent that numerous prior Indiana cases could affect the outcome. Tribe had to be familiar with all of them, and of course he was. I gradually learned, however, that he not only had a command of these cases, but also had read all the appellate briefs in all of these prior cases as well—and could discuss them in detail.

Tribe is not a trial lawyer, but you get the point. It is no coincidence that the hardest worker often delivers the most brilliant advocacy. We've all seen the bumper sticker that says, "I'd rather be sailing." If anyone does a bumper sticker for trial lawyers, it should probably say, "I'd rather be plowing through documents and reading arcane technical articles, so I can impeach the other side's expert." Which brings me to my next point.

## You'd Better Love It

Everyone approaches trial with a mixture of excitement, anxiety, fear, and dread. Everyone. Before, during, and after trial, the work is physically, mentally, and emotionally difficult. Emotional, mental, and physical difficulty; anxiety, fear, and dread. We usually don't think of these as positive things.

With respect to personal relationships, I don't know what to think of Charlotte's claim in *The Wild Palms* that love and suffering are the same thing. There certainly seems to be some truth in it. But if that notion is applied to trial work, I think she is right.

If you have what it takes to be a trial lawyer, you will love the emotional, mental, and physical difficulty, the anxiety, fear, and dread that come with trying cases. An experience most people would consider ghastly draws you in. In short, if you love the suffering that goes with trying cases, you probably have what it takes. Most people, for good reason, don't.

We have all seen brilliant, articulate, promising trial lawyers in their thirties who stopped trying cases by their forties. There are too many to count. They had everything needed for the job except the most important ingredient—the love of the suffering, the emotional resilience.

So try some cases. Then try some more. If, over time, it feels as if you are forcing yourself to do something you don't really want to do, give it up. Make your contribution to the world in some other way. Be proud that you are honest enough to not live up to someone else's idea of what a lawyer—or a person—should be. If, on the other hand, you find you are enjoying the process, even though that seems perverse in light how miserable it makes you, you probably have a long career as a trial lawyer ahead of you.

## You Will Still Hate It

No matter how well suited you are to the path of a trial lawyer, you will hate the job at times. There is no way around it. It might be on the Fourth of July weekend, when everyone you know is relaxing and having fun with their families, and you are working to prepare for depositions the following week. It might be at 11:00 P.M., as you work to finish the opposition to the seventh frivolous—but deceptively appealing—defense motion filed in your trial. It may be some sunny afternoon while you are trapped in a conference room listening to defense counsel question your fifty-five-year-old client about what drugs he took in high school. It may be during the third week of trial when you haven't slept for more than four consecutive hours in weeks.

At times, you will be fed up with the haggling, quibbling, and endless work. Everything is a fight, it seems, no matter how simple and straightforward the issue should be. The efforts of the defense to reduce the human condition to its lowest level, to appeal to the very worst in judges and juries, create a feeling of nausea and fatigue that won't go away. This does not necessarily mean you are ill-suited for being a trial lawyer; it may just mean you are a decent human being.

These feelings of disgust can last for hours, days, or months. With any luck, they will be interrupted by the euphoric feelings of joy, creative expression, and deep satisfaction this job can bring.

# CHAPTER FIVE

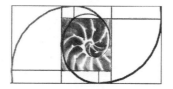

# Your First Trial

Lawyers have no established standards for determining when someone is ready to try a case. As you wrestle with the question of whether you are ready, remember that this awkward situation is not a result of any inadequacy on your part—the profession has let you down.

How do you know when you are ready for your first trial, your first murder trial, your first serious injury case? Some lawyers say the way to prepare is to second-chair several complex trials before attempting the simplest trial on your own. Others scoff at the second-chair approach and claim the best preparation is to start with the simplest cases and handle them on your own. Some say you must have ten felony trials under your belt before handling a murder case. Others will say that a murder case is simpler than some of the messier, lesser felonies—such as those relating to sexual abuse.

Most trial lawyers have strong opinions about what constitutes adequate background to try a particular type of case. Not surprising, most of them believe the way they obtained their experience is the preferable approach. The fact remains: there is no "standard of care" here.

If a lawyer you admire is willing to let you second-chair, take the offer. However, choose your mentor wisely—a bad first chair will leave you with bad experiences and bad habits.

Accept that your first several trials might be excruciatingly uncomfortable—no matter what the circumstances. You will make mistakes. That is unavoidable. It is also forgivable, as long as the mistakes are not born of arrogance or laziness.

Try not to get yourself into a position where your mistakes can do serious harm. With a good first chair, your client should be reasonably safe. If you are handling a case in which the stakes are relatively small, again, your client should be reasonably safe.

However, *relatively small* to you could be very important to your client. Don't try to conceal your lack of experience. Don't be afraid to say, "If I take this case, it will be my first drunk-driving case. Therefore, I will charge you half the going rate." You might say, "I have never handled a personal injury case of this size before, so if it goes to trial, I will bring in another, more experienced lawyer to help me try the case—at no extra cost to you." You may lose some clients this way, but not many. Most will appreciate your honesty, and you will communicate how important their case is to you. All clients want their case to be important to their lawyers. If they know it is your first case of this type, they will assume it is important to you, unless your conduct shows them otherwise.

If you are a new lawyer, your trial opportunities will mostly involve cases too small or too "unwinnable" for anyone else. You are the lawyer of last resort. If you are brave and work hard, you might prove the small case bigger than anyone thought or bring the unwinnable case to successful conclusion. And your client will have someone fighting for his best interests—often a first for our clients. This can be the most lasting gift we give our clients.

Almost all trial lawyers—no matter how accomplished—are insecure about their trial skills. The likelihood is that you will always be somewhat insecure about yours. This does not have to be a bad thing. It is what keeps you up nights researching the other side's expert or fine-tuning your *voir dire* questions. It is only a bad thing if it keeps you paralyzed, unable to get your trial feet wet. Some prefer to plunge in all at once; others prefer to get their toes wet, then their ankles, and so on. There is no single right way. Do what feels most comfortable. But keep getting wet.

# CHAPTER SIX

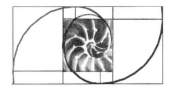

# Beyond Technique

I once read an article about a famous Hollywood actor. He was known for being the consummate lover, having had intimate encounters with almost every major actress over the previous thirty years. For some reason, many of these actresses were willing to give interviews to a national magazine and describe the details of their relations with him. Several of the actresses commented on this actor's careful, attentive, highly refined lovemaking technique. One concluded by saying something like, "But having sex with him was like holding on to a rubber life raft in a cold and turbulent sea."[4] This was not a compliment.

In human relations—and trial involves nothing if not human relations—technique is important. Think of teachers, therapists, stand-up comics, or singers. The good ones all study techniques in their fields to improve their effectiveness. In each of these fields, however, much more is going on than good technique. The singers with the best vocal technique are not necessarily the most popular or the ones who move us. Often the ones with poor technique can somehow reach out and grab us.

---

4. Now watch how virtually anything can be helpful in understanding trial practice.

The same is true of trial work. Lawyers with nearly flawless technique can lose case after case, while lawyers who appear clumsy and bumbling can win repeatedly.

Technique can be thought of as the product of experience and inspiration. Hundreds of years ago, after conducting numerous cross-examinations, some lawyer figured out that asking only leading questions (those to which he already knew the answers) brought the ability to control the story the witness told. A technique was born. Over time, the technique became dogma. Like most dogma, it provided structure and support, but also stifled spontaneity and creativity.

Trial lore is filled with stories of sloppy lawyers who paid a high price for asking nonleading questions on cross-examination. Trial lore is also filled with stories of inspired lawyers who dared to deviate from the dogma and scored huge points.

Don't think for a minute that I am denigrating technique. Techniques are your weapons. Study, save, and treasure them like any weapon you might depend on. Practice them until they become second nature. However, much teaching of trial practice loses sight of a significant truth: the weapon is less important than the person who chooses and wields it.

Outstanding teachers, singers, lovers, and trial lawyers have one thing in common: they communicate a truth that resonates inside them. They are trying to get that truth to resonate with their students, audience, lovers, or juries. Techniques are some of the tools available to aid their communication. How do they find that truth? How do they refine that truth? How do they keep other parts of their makeup from sabotaging that truth? This book attempts to address these questions—at least for trial lawyers.

Technique alone will not get you where you want to go. It will leave the jury—and perhaps you—"Holding on to a rubber life raft in a cold and turbulent sea." To be a good trial lawyer, be willing and able to give yourself to the jury. Not the self you wish you were or the self you think the jury might wish you were, but your actual self, the part of you that is scared, angry, or tired *and* the part of you that feels the justness of your case.

Most lawyers can't—or don't want to—do this. Showing jurors your real self is too scary. If you show them your real self, and they decide against you, they are rejecting not just your client—but you. Much safer to show them "Mr. Trial Lawyer" or "Ms. Smart Professional Woman." If you lose the case, at least *you* aren't being rejected, dismissed, squashed.

I'm not advocating temper tantrums, tears, or runaway emotions in the courtroom. Trying cases requires tremendous emotional discipline. An overdone emotion at the wrong time (and I'm tempted to say at any time) will kill your case. But let the jury see the case matters to you, that you believe in it heart and soul with nothing held back, and that can make all the difference. No protective cynicism or irony, no deft razzle-dazzle. Just you and your soul, out in the open, for all to see.

Doing this can feel as if you are tearing out your heart and putting it on the jury rail. You are in effect saying, "Here is my heart. Please don't crush it." If you lose after that, it is devastating. I have heard other longtime trial lawyers try to describe this feeling. It is a very personal thing. It makes all of us afraid.

In at least ten difficult cases in my life, I am convinced my willingness to expose myself in this way is all that won the trial. Working extremely hard and applying every ounce of skill I could muster did nothing but make it a close case. At closing, the case still hung in the balance. Something more was required, something harder to deliver—my vulnerability. I had to make a leap of faith to get the jury to leap with me.

Letting another person see who you really are is difficult. It can be terrifying. We all gravitate toward protective masks and behaviors. The higher the stress, the higher the stakes, the more we are inclined to present something other than our true selves to the outside world. The protective masks and behaviors make us feel safe.

The problem is that most people—including jurors—recognize these protective masks and behaviors. You are not fooling any-one—it just feels as though you are. They may not read your mind or your heart, but they'll know something isn't right—and assume the worst.

As with most trial skills, you can practice this outside the court-room. Try letting your spouse or your children see the parts of your-self you would just as soon keep hidden. Make yourself vulnerable to a friend or sibling by talking about something you would rather keep private. As you practice disclosing yourself to others, you will gain confidence and get more comfortable being your true self in a variety of situations, including inside the courtroom.

# CHAPTER SEVEN

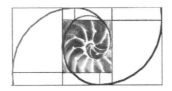

# You and Your Opponents

Chances are, you spend more time with your professional opponents than with your professional friends. You are with your opponents in endless depositions, in empty hallways before hearings, and constantly on the phone. Of course, if you are trying cases, you spend hour after emotion-charged hour in the courtroom with them.

At the beginning of this book, I said I would try to warn you of the traps that await you in the jungle of trial practice. A particularly dangerous trap is our relationship with our opponents. It is quicksand. Without the right attitude and approach, we are in danger of becoming angry, bitter, and foolish. If we let their behavior control the quality of our lives, we will likely be miserable much of the time.

This chapter attempts to help you deal with your opponents' bad behavior. The key is to step back from the day-to-day frustrations and annoyances they inflict upon you and evaluate who they really are. If you understand them better, you can better handle their behavior.

Let's talk first about civil defense lawyers, then prosecutors.

Disclaimer: I am describing psychological characteristics and tendencies commonly found in these groups of people. Here my purpose is not to accurately describe any particular person, but to help you deal with the generic bad behavior people in these roles may exhibit. Some civil defense lawyers and prosecutors are fine people and share none of the characteristics I describe. On the other hand, I believe you will recognize these characteristics in the people responsible for most of the bad behavior.

## Civil Defense Lawyers

Civil defense lawyers went to the best law schools, got the best grades, work in luxurious offices, and belong to the best clubs. They wear dark, expensive suits and self-satisfied expressions. The judges are their friends. They are powerful and in control; they rule the legal world. They don't doubt their entitlement to this position of power.

They also frequently engage in some or all of the following bad behavior:

- Bullying
- Dishonesty
- Stonewalling
- Failure to cooperate on scheduling and minor, nonsubstantive matters
- Frivolous discovery requests and motions
- Rude or condescending remarks
- Unwarranted accusations that your client is malingering
- Unwarranted accusations that you are engaging in unethical behavior

This bad behavior drives us crazy. Of course it does. I'm not saying it shouldn't. But if you understand what's behind this behavior, you can more easily deal with it on both a tactical and emotional level.

After long decades of observing defense lawyers in all sorts of situations, I am here to tell you what is behind most—though not all—of their bad behavior. They envy you, they fear you, and they resent you. Yes, *you,* the guy who got a D in Civil Procedure, the woman who can't stand in front of a jury without shaking uncontrollably, the one who lies awake nights wondering how to pay next month's rent.

To understand how this can be, you must imagine how defense lawyers experience life and how your life looks to them. They sell their time (and sometimes it feels like their souls) in six-minute increments. They have to answer to their partners, their clients, and even their clients' accountants for every six minutes of their lives. No matter how much they are paid per hour, they are slaves to the clock. Their partners pressure them to bill as many hours as possible; their advancement within the firm and yearly income depend upon it. Their clients give them countervailing pressure to be efficient and keep the hours they work on a case to a minimum. Every month (or quarter), they must send a report justifying everything they did on a case and everything they plan to do in the future. They do not get to bill for preparing these reports. They sweated their way through college and law school for this?

Moreover, their corporate masters have a win-at-any-cost attitude, which they are expected to share. If they lose, there is hell to pay. If they win, the home office still puts their bill under a microscope.

You, they believe, don't answer to anyone. You come and go as you wish. Your clients are unsophisticated and will do whatever you tell them to do. You don't keep time slips. You write a demand letter or two, and the insurance company sends you a check. You get to keep a third, whether you did any real work on the case or not.

And yes, they know you're the one in law-school class who got the D in Civil Procedure.

They have seen it over and over again. Some mediocre plaintiff's lawyer gets a quadriplegic client with slam-dunk liability and is financially set for life. Even if this hasn't happened to *you,* the defense lawyers believe it can at any time. Meanwhile, the most they can look forward to is a higher hourly rate, with the closer scrutiny from partners and clients that comes with it.

Worst of all, they've been culturally typecast as the bad guy. They feel they do the mature, responsible thing in helping the productive engines of society run smoothly and efficiently. They defend the castle against the mob of villagers with pitchforks and torches. They should be regarded as heroes, protecting the values of our free-enterprise society—but they're not.

Civil defense lawyers believe in their heart that plaintiff's lawyers don't care about their clients and are only in it for the money. They, on the other hand, believe they are trying to live by larger values—but are unfairly viewed as corporate lackeys who will do anything for money—even go to war against widows, orphans, and the handicapped. Civil defense lawyers know in their heart they are good, humane people; they resent the fact they are regarded as villains. Still, deep down they recognize there is nothing heroic about what they do.

Being typecast as the bad guy is troublesome enough for male lawyers, but for female lawyers the problem is even worse. Villains who beat up on the disadvantaged are often seen as masculine—in the same way Darth Vader is masculine. But in our culture, battling widows, orphans, and the handicapped is the antithesis of femininity. Female civil defense lawyers have no way around this. The more successful they are at undermining the claims of the disadvantaged, the more they undermine their own feminine identity in our culture.

These factors help explain the envy and resentment. What about fear? Can it possibly be that these powerful people fear *you?* Yes.

First, anyone with any sense fears *any* opponent. In our business, on the right day, with the right set of circumstances, a rookie can beat a master. Second, and more important, you have done some things they haven't done or can't do, and that causes them to fear you.

You are in a small firm, with no guarantee of clients or income. You have no structure for support; you don't travel in a herd. The very things that vex defense lawyers—time slips, micromanaging adjusters, and quarterly reports—also comfort them. Without those things, they would have to stand on their own, as you do. The way you live your professional life and the risks you encounter on a daily basis show defense lawyers you are capable of something they believe is beyond them. More than that, it terrifies them. Deep down, they don't understand how you can do it. They know you must have something they don't, and that is frightening.

Just as a dog fears a coyote half its size, defense lawyers fear you. You have no collar, no fence, and no warm place to sleep at night.

When dealing with you, defense lawyers experience envy, resentment, and fear. Is it any wonder that many act like miserable human beings during litigation?

After spending the last few pages giving you my pop-psychological explanation for defense attorneys' bad behavior, let me freely admit I may be wrong. There are certainly individual defense attorneys whose bad behavior is not motivated by the forces I've described. Even as gross generalizations, my observations may be off the mark. (I don't think so, but you should judge for yourself.) In a way, that is immaterial. My point is this: in the context of litigation, you and defense counsel are two different species.

As any two humans, you and defense counsel have much in common. You love your children; you feel pain and hunger; you struggle with humanity's issues of life, death, and meaning. You may even share common interests, like the Boston Red Sox or model trains. But in the litigation arena, you are different species with some similar traits. Faced with similar stimuli, you and defense counsel will respond differently, just as the coyote and the dog will respond differently to the same situation. This is because your psychological landscapes, as they relate to litigation, are fundamentally different.

So what? So it is important to remember this when dealing with defense attorneys, or they will drive you crazy.

When defense lawyers repeatedly make frivolous, coaching objections in a deposition, it is easy to get upset. They are breaking the rules, acting like a nervous French poodle out on the prairie—barking and yipping at every little insect. If they wear a smug, superior expression while doing it, or if they try to bully you with loud personal attacks, it's hard not to engage them on an emotional level.

You need to remember that this type of behavior is a reflection on *them,* not on *you.* They are just doing what anxious, resentful, envious defense attorneys do. Getting into the emotional muck with them gets you nowhere. Like most dysfunctional people, they only become more comfortable as you get more dysfunctional or emotional yourself. If you sink to their level, your case will sink with you.

To illustrate, let's take a common scenario I think of as the "picador technique." The picador is the man on horseback who throws spears into the back of the bull before the matador shows up to fight the bull. By the time the matador enters the ring, the bull is tired and enraged from dealing with the picador. Even for a bull, he now has poor judgment, charging at the red cape while the matador coolly and calmly steps aside.

Many defense lawyers, consciously or unconsciously, use this same technique. Outside the courtroom, they repeatedly torment the plaintiff's counsel. By the time the two attorneys step into court together, the plaintiff's counsel is like the enraged bull, charging and snorting at the slightest provocation. In contrast, the defense lawyer has become the calm, mild-mannered matador. Could he possibly give offense to anyone? The plaintiff's counsel charges and snorts around the courtroom, forgetting that neither the judge nor the jury has seen the defense counsel's true colors. The plaintiff's counsel looks out of control and unreasonable; the defense counsel looks calm and reliable. Another plaintiff's case is lost.

You are a professional. You are in court, in deposition, or on the phone to do a job. Your job is to advance your client's cause and ultimately win the case. Getting into an emotional relationship with defense counsel undermines your ability to do your job.

Uncomfortable with metaphors about dogs and coyotes or matadors and bulls? Then consider the Spartans from ancient Greece and their attitude toward adversaries:

> *The Spartans are schooled to regard the foe, any foe, as nameless and faceless. In their minds it is the mark of an ill-prepared and amateur army to rely in the moments before battle on what they call pseudoandreia, false courage, meaning the artificially inflated martial frenzy produced by a general's eleventh-hour harangue or some peak of bronze-banging bravado built to by shouting, shield-pounding and the like.[5]*

Here is a description of several thousand Spartans facing a larger enemy force across an open field.

---

5. Steven Pressfield, *Gates of Fire* (Doubleday, 1998), 87.

*Now the clamor began.*

*Among the enemy's ranks, the bravest (or perhaps the most fear-stricken) began banging the ash of their spear shafts upon the bronze bowls of their shields, creating a tumult of pseudoandreia which reverberated across and around the mountain-enclosed plain. Others reinforced this racket with the warlike thrusting of their spear-points to heaven and the loosing of cries to the gods and shouts of threat and anger. The roar multiplied threefold, then five, and then ten, as the enemy rear ranks and flankers picked the clamor up and contributed their own bluster and bronze-banging. Soon the entire fifty-four hundred were bellowing the war cry. Their commander thrust his spear forward and the mass surged behind him into the advance.*

*The Spartans had neither moved nor made a sound.*

*They waited patiently in their scarlet-clad ranks, neither firm nor rigid, but speaking quietly to each other words of encouragement and cheer, securing the final preparation for actions they had rehearsed hundreds of times in training and performed dozens and scores more in battle.*[6]

This passage goes on to describe the terrifying effect the Spartans' calm had on the enemy and how the Spartans' detachment gave them the advantage in the heat of battle.

---

6. Pressfield, *Gates of Fire*, 101.

Let defense lawyers pound their shields and bellow their war cries. You are the detached Spartan, above and beyond your opponent's emotions.

Inertia favors the defense. You have to motivate the judge or the jury to want to do something. If, to the judge or the jury, your case is mostly a spite fight between two attorneys, *you lose*. Only if the issues are larger and more important do you have a chance to motivate the decision makers. Rule breaking by defense counsel may wind you up, but it will rarely make any impression on a judge or jury.

If you accept my hypothesis that most of defense counsel's bad behavior is a product of envy, resentment, or fear of you, you can more easily stay emotionally detached. If you stay detached, I believe you will see more evidence in support of my hypothesis. Most important, emotional detachment from defense counsel allows you to do your job more effectively and reduces your stress level. Simply stated, you signed up for a job dealing with high-strung, nervous French poodles. You are never going to have a warm and fuzzy relationship with these dogs. Sometimes you may be able to stop them from yipping and yapping, other times not. Your job is to win the case, not stop the yapping. The case and the yapping are almost always two entirely separate things.

Finally, I am not suggesting you always put up with bad behavior, but that sometimes you should. Ask yourself if the behavior is going to influence the outcome of the case. If not, you may want to let it speak for itself. If it might affect the outcome of the case, your best course is almost always to dispassionately record or report the bad behavior. Don't let the issue become about you or your emotions.

# Prosecutors

Three main types of prosecutors usually commit bad behavior:

1. The ambitious, self-centered type
2. The moral or authoritarian type
3. The need-for-power type

All prosecutors (and people) have aspects of these traits in their personalities. Too strong a dose, however, can lead the prosecutor to unfair decisions and improper tactics.

## AMBITIOUS, SELF-CENTERED PROSECUTORS

For ambitious, self-centered prosecutors, the criminal justice system is a stage designed to show them to their best advantage. Although these prosecutors may wrap themselves in a cloak of public service, they always have one eye on their resume and the other on the local newspaper or television station. With no particular allegiance to fair play or the principles underlying our criminal justice system, these prosecutors behave badly if they believe their conduct will advance their career or win the approval of peers, superiors, or the public. For ambitious, self-centered prosecutors, you are just an extra in a movie about *them*.

## MORAL OR AUTHORITARIAN PROSECUTORS

The main concern of moral or authoritarian prosecutors is always being right. Emotionally, that is where they feel safe—the *only* place they feel safe. Ambiguity and shades of gray cause them high anxiety. They are on the side of right, fighting against criminals. They *are* the government, fighting against criminals. The criminals are *bad*. They are *good*. You represent the criminals; that makes you *bad*. Only a chump would play fairly when dealing with the bad guys. The end justifies the means.

To moral or authoritarian prosecutors, all defense lawyers are morally infirm—though some are worse than others. They may not say it; they may not even think it; but they feel this down to their bones.

## NEED-FOR-POWER PROSECUTORS

To need-for-power prosecutors, the exercise of power over others is an end in itself. It is what lets these prosecutors know they are alive, they are important, and their life has meaning. Seeing you beg for a deal for your client gives them a thrill. Bullying witnesses and defendants also gives them a thrill. That is enough for them. Need-for-power prosecutors view any of your actions in representing your client as a challenge to their power or authority.

You may have things in common with any of these prosecutors. You may share interests in the New York Yankees or books by Laura Ingalls Wilder. What should be clear, however, is that you shouldn't exchange intimacies or emotions with them. You have very different worldviews. When they act badly, they do so for reasons that have nothing to do with you. What you think of their conduct matters little to them. They have no interest in understanding you or your values.

When they act badly, it can have catastrophic consequences for your client. You need to police these prosecutors and make them follow the rules. In the end, however, your objective is to shepherd your client through the justice system and achieve the best result you can. Feuding with prosecutors or expressing your moral indignation to judges or juries rarely helps achieve that goal.

## The Double Standard

Here is an essential point you must always remember: civil defense lawyers and prosecutors can get away with bad behavior that we cannot. Civil defense lawyers and prosecutors can be rude, dishonest, and comically incompetent and still win. We cannot be any of those things and still win.

Prosecutors can get away with this behavior because they represent the government. Cloaked with authority and presumed righteousness, prosecutors are given a pass by jurors. Jurors assume a prosecutor's conduct is justified, even if they don't understand it.

Civil defense lawyers get away with bad behavior, because when they demean the trial process, they automatically demean the plaintiff's case. If what the defense lawyer successfully conveys is, "This is just a game between lawyers" or "This whole process is unsavory," the plaintiff's verdict will not be good.

Our job as trial lawyers is to elevate the process and the discussion. We ask the jury to deal with important issues that affect not just the parties, but society as a whole. We must resist the temptation to fight fire with fire. The ugly tools that work for prosecutors and civil defense attorneys simply don't work for us.

# Part II

# Traps in the Jungle

*At the end of the day, no matter how confident we are in our observations, our experiments, our data, or our theories, we must go home knowing that 85 percent of all gravity in the cosmos comes from an unknown, mysterious source that remains completely undetected by all means we have ever devised to observe the universe.*

—Neil DeGrasse Tyson,
*Death by Black Hole and Other Cosmic Quandaries*

ALL TRIAL LAWYERS MAKE TECHNICAL MISTAKES. WE PREPARE A SLOPPY, disorganized *voir dire,* pursue a ridiculous line of cross-examination, or miss a legal issue that is staring us in the face. Usually, at least afterward, we can see what we did wrong and try to improve at our next opportunity.

Trial lawyers also make another category of mistakes. These mistakes are grounded in erroneous attitudes and assumptions. Even after we make them, these mistakes are not self-evident. They are reinforced by our legal and popular culture as well as by our own personal psychologies. As a result, we can walk into the same trap over and over again, all the while thinking our mistake is evidence of quality performance. This is our personal blind spot, our Achilles' heel.

All people have blind spots specific and peculiar to their own personalities. But certain mistaken attitudes and assumptions are so common among trial lawyers that they merit an entire book section. Here it is, Part II. This part includes the hidden traps many of us fall into over and over, usually without even realizing it. I can show you where the traps are; only you can protect yourself from falling in.

# CHAPTER EIGHT

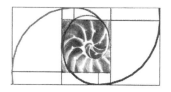

# Beware of Formulas

*To the scientist, the universality of physical laws makes the cosmos a marvelously simple place. By comparison, human nature—the psychologist's domain—is infinitely more daunting.*

—Neil DeGrasse Tyson,
*Death by Black Hole and Other Cosmic Quandaries*

It is human nature to seek understanding of the world in which we function and live. We study, we measure, we theorize, we label, all in a search for understanding. Understanding can make our lives easier, seemingly more predictable, and much less scary.

Once our scientists tell us that the earth is flat, then we know how to behave with respect to practical geographic matters. Perhaps more important, we have a framework for understanding our world and our place on it. With our understanding that the earth is flat comes the knowledge that the sun, moon, and stars revolve around the earth, which is the center of the universe. This understanding in turn informs our knowledge of God and humankind and how humankind should act here, in the center of the universe.

As Neil DeGrasse Tyson points out in *Death by Black Hole and Other Cosmic Quandaries*, the ancients had plenty of sound, scientific reasons to believe the earth was flat. These were not stupid people, but they were wrong. With limited knowledge and perspective and a strong desire to explain the scary, mysterious world in which they lived, they reached the wrong conclusion. As Tyson also points out, today, with all our advanced technology and data, our increase in understanding, although real, is barely perceptible when measured against all that we don't know. The same can be said for our knowledge of what goes on in a courtroom.

We have our experiences and observations, our pretrial focus groups and post-trial juror interviews, our social science experiments, and, more recently, our neuroscience studies. In the end, the interaction of forces and factors in the courtroom rivals in complexity those found in the vast reaches of the universe, and much of what happens in the courtroom remains—if we are honest with ourselves—unknown and mysterious.

This does not stop lawyers and jury consultants from seeking and proclaiming universal courtroom truths. Let's look at a few that have cropped up over the years:

- In *voir dire,* jurors of southern European ancestry are more likely to vote for the plaintiff in a civil case or the defendant in a criminal case than jurors of northern European ancestry. An Irish person is to be preferred over a Scot at all costs; the Irish are generous, the Scots are cheap.
- The jurors' demographics are most important. Age and occupation are critical. Engineers are worse than social workers; older people are better than younger.
- The jurors' personal experiences and value systems control their decisions.
- Ninety percent of all communication is nonverbal.

- Using neurolinguistic programming when presenting a case, for example, always standing in the same spot when making certain important points, can program the jurors to make the desired decision.
- Wearing brown conveys friendliness and credibility; wearing dark blue conveys authority.
- Jurors remember best what they hear first and last, called *primacy* and *recency*. One should always begin and end on the most important points, whether in opening, closing, or examining witnesses.

This brings us to a common problem among people trying to become better trial lawyers: thinking there are rules or formulas that are universally true in the courtroom. We think these rules—telling us which juror to strike, where to stand in the courtroom, and what suit to wear—will give us the one right answer for solving a particular advocacy problem.

There are no such rules or formulas. There never have been. There never will be. The process is too complex.

We all want a formula, don't we? We want so badly to do a good job. We want so badly to win. If an authority were to tell us we could win our cases by dressing in a mime suit and memorizing the first three books of the Old Testament, anyone reading this book would gladly do so. That would be much easier than what we actually have to do.

So we read Irving Younger's *Ten Commandments of Cross-examination* and try hard to follow his precepts to the letter. By calling them the "Ten Commandments," Younger implied we must always follow them, and when we do, everything will be okay. Many lawyers have strictly followed these commandments through one bad cross-examination after another.

This is not to say there isn't great wisdom in Younger's *Ten Commandments* or in many of the other principles advocated by those who study the trial process. It *is* to say that none of them are universal—that is, always controlling or true.

You can best understand these principles as forces that can influence the outcome of a trial. Each principle, assuming it is true, can help influence the outcome—but it doesn't act alone. An unimaginable number of other principles or forces are also at work, interacting with each other to produce a verdict. Let's look at some examples to help understand this point.

All students of advocacy, from Aristotle to the most up-to-date jury consultant, agree that the advocate's credibility is critically important in persuading a jury. The more the advocate appears to be an honest person of good character and common sense, the more receptive the jurors are to his or her message.

The late Al Julien, an enormously talented and successful plaintiff's lawyer from New York City, tells of being asked to represent a client in a particularly anti-Semitic area of upstate New York. At first he refused, knowing that a Jew from New York City would have no credibility with the upstate jurors. When the client insisted, Julien agreed, on the condition that the client would allow him to try the case as he wished, with no questions asked.

At trial, Julien performed horribly, stumbling over himself, forgetting his points, and losing exhibits. The famously fast-talking Jew could hardly string two sentences together. The client was astonished when he received a substantial verdict. The jurors told him they felt sorry for him, because he had "that incompetent Jew lawyer," and they stepped in to make sure justice was done.[7] Lacking any hope of being credible with the jury, Julien was able to invoke

7. Al Julien, *Opening Statements* (Callaghan, 1986).

72

other available forces that affect outcome in the courtroom.

The point here is not that you should squander your credibility in the courtroom, but that all forces, no matter how powerful, interact with a myriad of others to produce a verdict. If our focus is on mastering a predictive science, this is bad news. If we are concerned with winning cases that appear difficult or impossible, this is good news. It tells us that courage, creativity, and adaptability can go a long way toward winning difficult cases.

Let's look at how three forces or principles might interact. Younger's Eighth Commandment is, "Disallow witness explanation." In other words, don't allow witnesses to explain their answers. The concept here is that, in explaining their answers, witnesses may rehabilitate themselves. One of the forces operating in the courtroom is the tendency of witnesses to try to defend themselves by giving the best explanation they can. Another operating force is that the trial lawyer can never know everything and, so, can never know what might come out of a witness's mouth. The Eighth Commandment teaches respect for these forces.

We also know that a great deal of communication (though probably not 90 percent) is nonverbal. All of us, including jurors, judge others by their tone and how they look as well as by their actual words. When a witness gives an improbable answer on cross-examination, the Eighth Commandment says not to allow an explanation. But if the witness is looking bad—in a nonverbal sense—it may be more effective to let the witness keep talking and let the jury continue to experience the nonverbal messages the witness is sending out. Every experienced trial lawyer has violated the Eighth Commandment to great effect on some occasions.

Let's look at one last example—the forces of primacy and recency. Social science has pretty well established that it is easiest for people to remember the first and last information they hear in a particular situation. However, if we present a boring or unimportant piece of information first or last, the rules of primacy and recency do not mean listeners will remember this information. And if they do remember it, it will not necessarily influence their decision making. This force, or rule, simply tells us how to make our information more accessible to the jury.

Good trial lawyers learn about such concepts as primacy and recency and the Ten Commandments and respect them as representative of forces operating in the courtroom. These lawyers understand that none of these forces control across all cases or situations. They understand that even powerful forces may be cancelled by others. Their job is to learn what they can about these forces and harness them the best they can for their client. Ultimately, the harnessing of these forces is an art, not a science—but science, especially social science, can provide great assistance.

A major challenge for trial lawyers is to identify and separate legitimate courtroom forces from those that are not really forces at all. Trial lawyers will never learn much about the universe of the courtroom if they believe the earth is flat. Yet, just as astrophysicists must understand why intelligent people from earlier times believed the earth was flat, trial lawyers must learn and understand the teachings of those who came before them, before they can learn what to keep and what to discard.

I am reminded of the story about the man who was ordered to carve an elephant out of a giant block of granite. He had a hammer and chisel. When he protested that he did not know how to carve an elephant, he was told to simply carve away everything that did not look like an elephant. I may not be able to show you the elephant, but here in Part II, I hope to help you start carving away at the granite.

CHAPTER NINE

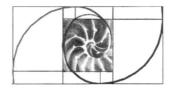

# Do Not Expect Perfection

You are about to start your trial. You've visualized this moment for weeks, months, or even years. It's perfectly choreographed in your head. You've worked tirelessly to make sure every contingency is covered. You've gone to CLE sessions on *voir dire,* opening, direct examination, cross-examination, and closing. You've watched the best trial lawyers in the country demonstrate effective techniques. You are ready.

In your mind's eye, the trial will be a cross between a forensic firestorm and a beautiful ballet, wondrous to behold. The judge walks into the courtroom, everyone rises, and within five minutes your beautiful ballet has turned into mud wrestling.

Maybe the judge changes his mind; yesterday he granted forty-five minutes for opening statements, but now he says you have twenty. He won't let you use your exhibits in opening. A jury panelist gives an answer in *voir dire* that seems to gut your case and leaves everyone in the courtroom laughing at you. The judge grants a motion to exclude your best evidence. The defense lawyer gives an argument you didn't anticipate based on evidence you were not aware existed.

Deviation from your imagined ballet does not necessarily mean something has gone wrong. It is also possible that the defense makes an admission, a witness makes an offhand comment, or the judge makes a ruling that unexpectedly helps your case. Since these opportunities were not part of your trial plan, you may not even notice them. You could waste them if you single-mindedly focus on the trial you planned to conduct and don't recognize the gift you've been given.

Every minute of trial presents an opportunity for the unexpected to present itself. You may actually be a pretty good mud wrestler, but have that ballet stuck in your head. Every move makes you painfully aware of the gap between what you expected the trial to be and what it actually is. Your self-conscious awareness of that gap is more likely to be your undoing than whatever it is you think has gone wrong.

Let's look first at where these expectations come from, then at how they interfere with effective performance at trial. Finally, let's look at how to use them to your advantage while moving beyond them.

## Where Do Expectations Come From?

It's easy to see where we get our expectations, isn't it? Read a book on trial practice, and it contains examples of how to perform *voir dire*, opening, or any of the other components of trial. Chances are, the author spent many hours making up the questions and answers or modifying an actual transcript to convey exactly how he or she thinks a perfect trial should go.

Go to a CLE seminar, and some of the best lawyers in the country are there. They are well rested, well prepared, and giving a short presentation in a very controlled environment. Their set-piece closing argument looks flawless. Of course it does. Read enough trial practice books, attend enough CLE seminars, and you begin to think that what you read and see there represents the reality of how a trial should go.

# How Expectations Interfere with Performance

If you constantly compare how the trial *should be* going with how it actually *is* going, you are on a different wavelength than everyone else in the courtroom. With your mind engaged in comparisons, you compromise your ability to accurately perceive what is actually going on. We are all familiar with the phenomenon in other contexts.

Perhaps you planned a date with your husband. You made reservations at a restaurant your friends have been raving about; you plan to follow up with a movie you're both eager to see. All week the two of you talk about how much you are looking forward to your date on Friday.

You arrive at the restaurant. They don't have a record of your reservation, and they have no room for you. You rush to another restaurant about five blocks away and, after a brief wait, are able to get in. As you eat your meal, you repeatedly replay in your mind how the mix-up with the reservation could have happened; you constantly compare the food, service, and atmosphere with those at the restaurant where you'd hoped to eat. Of course, if you do that, you are almost guaranteed to have a miserable time.

If you put the ideal restaurant behind you and focus on the here and now with your husband, you might not only have a good time, but you might have a better time than you otherwise would have. Maybe the new restaurant starts a line of conversation between you that continues long into the evening. You both enjoy it so much you decide to skip the movie. Instead, you go for a walk through the park and bump into old friends you haven't seen in years.

Most of us are disappointed when a date doesn't go as we planned, but most of us are mature enough to shift our attention from where we had planned to be to where we actually are. We are able to do this, in part, because we are not reading books and attending seminars telling us that, to have an enjoyable date with our spouse, we *must* only be at a certain restaurant, dressed in particular clothes, eating only specific foods, at specific times.

If you make it your business to read great trial lawyers' transcripts and to watch them in actual trials, you will learn, as I have, that things constantly go wrong for them too. Judges rule against them, witnesses give unexpected and damaging answers, and these great lawyers lose their train of thought. However, they are not self-conscious about it. They are not concerned with looking good; they are concerned with winning. I don't think I have ever seen a great trial lawyer who was a perfectionist at trial.

As a personal aside, I note that some of my most artful cross-examinations left almost no impression on the jury; some of my sloppiest devastated the defense. I gave some of my most eloquent closing arguments in cases I lost, and some of my largest verdicts came after closing arguments I would be embarrassed to have anyone review.

## Use and Move Beyond Expectations

If something goes wrong on our date, we know that if we insist on trying to have our perfect date, things will just keep getting worse. The same is true in trial. The more we try to hold to our original vision of perfection, the worse things get.

That does not mean you should not plan and have expectations. Although great trial lawyers are not perfectionists *at* trial, they are usually perfectionists *before* trial. They prepare and prepare, and then prepare some more. Extensive preparation lets them confidently shift from one tactic to another while the trial unfolds.

Steer a course between two extremes. Some lawyers prepare and plan and then cannot let go of their plans, even when they no longer make sense in the context of the trial that is actually going on. Other lawyers shoot from the hip without much thought or preparation— and they lose cases they should win.

Please understand, I am not suggesting you abandon your game plan at the first sign of trouble. Nor am I suggesting you not strive to make every part of your performance at trial as artful and effective as you can. Your game plan represents your best thinking about how you should try the case. Books and CLE seminars give you a standard of performance worth aspiring to. However, when the gavel pounds and everybody rises, it's time to cast off the burden of your expectations.

# CHAPTER TEN

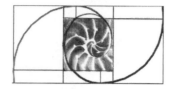

# Forget Playing It Safe

We all are taught from childhood to play it safe in social situations. We are taught not to express opinions that might be controversial or offend others. By adulthood, we typically don't express an opinion among strangers unless it is of the blandest, most mundane sort ("I hate this rain, don't you?").

The way to play it safe in law school was to raise and explain every possible issue. If five arguments supported a particular result, you had better discuss them all.

All of this training works against you at trial. *There is no safe way to try a case—unless you are a prosecutor or civil defense lawyer.* Representing people at trial is not like designing a bridge or flying a plane. To do it right, you have to take risks. The two main ways lawyers avoid these risks are by playing it safe tactically and playing it safe psychologically—although I believe in all cases it is mostly psychological risk we seek to avoid.

## Playing It Safe Tactically

Let's talk about a few common tactical risks that confront trial lawyers. Your client has a claim for injury to his leg. Your state allows recovery for emotional and mental distress for that injury, and your complaint requests damages for emotional and mental distress. Your client also has a long history of psychological care, including references to delusional behavior and his beating his wife. If you drop the emotional and mental distress claim, the defense is either not allowed discovery of the psychological history or the court will rule it inadmissible.

There is no safe way of handling this situation. Most lawyers—especially new ones—feel safer maintaining the emotional distress claim. That seems the way to get the most money—more claims equal more money. The client can't later criticize you by pointing to an article in a newspaper in which someone recovered $1 million for mental and emotional distress associated with a similar injury.

As you sit in trial, however, watching the jurors' disgusted reactions to your client's psychological history, you may have second thoughts. But if you think dropping the emotional distress claim is safe, think again. The judge may admit reference to your client's psychological history, even if that shouldn't have been allowed. The defense may come up with an independent reason that makes the history relevant. You have then dropped a claim for no good reason, or so it may seem to an armchair trial lawyer.

How about making objections during trial? Do you make the objections to "preserve the record" on appeal and risk incurring the jury's distrust, even wrath? Alternatively, do you let the opposition's impropriety go without objection, losing the chance to appeal the issue and knowing you can be criticized later for not objecting to obvious legal errors?

As a criminal defense lawyer, do you put your client on the stand to tell his story, or do you rely on his Fifth Amendment right to stay silent?

Anyone who tells you there is only one right way to handle these situations is giving you bad advice. In a particular case, there may be only one right way to handle an issue, but that does not mean the same approach is right for the next case. The truth is, the choice may be between two bad choices, each of which can cause its own brand of trouble.

All tactical decisions, almost by definition, involve some risk, whatever choice you make. When I talk with lawyers wrestling with these types of tactical decisions, I notice two common themes:

1. Many are trying to find the safest tactical decision—by which I mean the decision that will make them *feel* safe.

2. Many are consciously or unconsciously trying to make a decision that will not leave them open to others' criticism.

As for the first theme, you might as well get used to the fact that a tactical decision will seldom feel safe. At trial, we make a series of choices between a series of risky alternatives. That is a big part of our job description. For example, you may have every reason to think your criminal defendant will do a good job as a witness and put her on the stand. Still, no matter how good a witness she turns out to be, you will never, ever feel safe while she is testifying—or in the days leading up to her testimony. Conversely, if you decide *not* to have her testify, that will often feel unsafe as well. It may feel less dangerous than having her testify, but it will almost never feel safe.

Some lawyers try to avoid choosing between unsafe choices by ignoring that there is a tactical decision to be made. Of course, you can't ignore some decisions—like whether to put your client on the stand. You can ignore other decisions if you pretend there is only one course of action—but that is making a *de facto* decision, isn't it?

In short, your job is to take calculated risks on behalf of your client. You may be certain you are making the right tactical choice, but I doubt you will ever feel safe. If you want to feel safe, find another job.

If you put your criminal defendant on the stand, she may fall apart. Does that mean you made the wrong decision? Not necessarily. It depends, in part, on what your chances of winning were without putting her on the stand. Nevertheless, someone who knows less about the case than you will undoubtedly offer criticism, no matter what you did, if the case goes badly.

This brings us to the second theme I repeatedly see in lawyers struggling with tactical decisions: looking for psychological safety in the approval of their peers. They intuitively know they can be criticized for any tactical decision if the case goes badly. So they try (consciously or unconsciously) to make the decision their peers would support.

These lawyers have one eye on the audience at all times—the audience of their imagined peers who will judge their decisions. The question shifts from, "What will maximize my client's chances of winning?" to "What would my peers think is the best course to take?" or "What is the conventional wisdom about this sort of tactical issue?" Let me first state the obvious: your peers know much less about the case than you. They also have no responsibility for the results— which has a way of making people much more convinced that they know the right course of action. Finally, "conventional wisdom" regarding trial practice is more about making lawyers feel safer than about helping them win cases.

In all tactical decisions, you give up something to gain something else. When you make these decisions, there is no safe route. In hindsight, you may have made the wrong decision. Or you may have made the right decision, but things still went wrong. You may have made the wrong decision, but won the case anyway. There is no safe decision;

they all involve risk—risk of hurting the case and risk of incurring others' criticism. There is no way around this. It is your job.

This is not to say that you should not ask for advice or consider conventional wisdom when confronting tactical choices. What it does mean is that your very human desire to insulate yourself from criticism has no place in your tactical decision making. When you make tactical trial decisions based on how you will look to others, you are selling out your client to protect your own ego. Big mistake.

So what *should* you do when making tactical decisions?

1. Think through the problem thoroughly on your own.

2. Brainstorm with your friends and partners to come up with as many courses of action as possible.

3. Weigh the pros and cons of the choices.

4. Continue weighing the pros and cons as the case evolves.

5. When you have to make a choice, base it on what you believe is in your client's best interests. Your job is to take calculated tactical risks on your client's behalf.

6. Accept the fact that you may look foolish for the choice you made. That is your job. If you are not willing to risk looking foolish, you have no business being a trial lawyer.

## Playing It Safe Psychologically

It should be clear from the previous discussion that playing it tactically safe comes from trying to play it psychologically safe. We want to feel safe and avoid criticism.

Other ways of playing it safe psychologically don't directly involve trial tactics. These are the mind games we play with ourselves to make the stress and uncertainty of trial easier to bear. Here are some of the more common ones. If you catch yourself doing one of these, you are chickening out. You are working to protect yourself instead of working to win the case.

1. **NOT CARING—ABOUT THE CASE OR THE CLIENT.** The pain of losing is too much to contemplate, maybe because you have experienced it too many times. Your reaction can range from cynical hostility ("I have a scumbag for a client anyway") to finely tuned irony ("Isn't it funny how everyone makes such a big fuss over a broken leg?"). One way or another, you communicate to yourself and those around you that you don't really care about the outcome of the case. You are too cool to care, too sophisticated to worry, really, too good for the case or the client.

   This attitude creeps up on people. Most don't intentionally adopt it. Watch out. If you start thinking or talking this way, you are working too hard at protecting yourself. You are like boxers or football players who are afraid of getting hit. They can't perform as they should if they're mostly concerned with protecting themselves—and neither can you.

2. **TELLING YOURSELF THE CASE CAN'T BE WON.** Look how hard it is. How could anyone expect you to win it? *No one* could win *this* case. If the case is hopeless, no one can blame you for losing—not your client, not your peers, not yourself. What are you doing when you start thinking like this? Playing it safe, protecting yourself again.

   Now, it is true that some cases *can't* be won, but still may need to be tried. Part of your job, I am sorry to say, is to convince yourself there is a way—no matter how improbable—that you can win the case. Do this for two reasons. First, you may be wrong in your evaluation. The case may be more winnable than you think or understand. Second, anything can happen in a trial—and it just might in this one. An unexpected opportunity may rear up in the courtroom and change things in an instant. If you've already succumbed to self-pity and decided there is no way to win, the opportunity may pass you by.

3. **KEEPING SCORE DURING THE TRIAL.** What I mean by this is rationalizing why you lost the case before the trial is even over. You keep a list of reasons you can present to yourself and others as to why you lost. You greet every adverse ruling with a mixed emotional reaction: disappointment that the case just got harder mixed with relief that you can point to something else to justify the loss. The same thing happens when a bad juror is seated or a witness testifies poorly. You play it psychologically safe by keeping a running list of each event, so that afterward you can point to the bad luck, bad judge, or bad juror who cost you the case.

4. **HOLDING BACK A PIECE OF YOURSELF.** All these ways of playing it safe have two things in common. The lawyers who do them are, first, trying to protect themselves from the psychological pain of losing and, second, holding back from a full psychological and emotional commitment to winning.

We all seek to protect ourselves from emotional pain. If you fully commit to winning, then losing is a devastating, miserable experience. It only makes sense to hold back a piece of yourself, to save yourself the pain, "just in case." The problem is that in doing so, you reduce your chances of winning. Again, a football player whose main priority is avoiding injury is unlikely to play as well as he otherwise would. The same is true of the trial lawyer. In protecting yourself, you miss opportunities to shine— intellectually and emotionally. And sometimes the only way to win is to shine.

This is certainly not an exhaustive list of ways in which trial lawyers try to play it safe psychologically. Chances are, you have some special techniques of your own. Watch for them. They undermine your success. Perhaps more important, they undermine the joy you can find in throwing yourself into something without reservation. Not many people ever find that in their jobs.

# CHAPTER ELEVEN

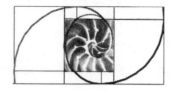

# More Is Not Better

*Perfection is not when there is no more to add, but no more to take away.*

—Antoine de Saint-Exupéry

When writing a law-school exam, more is almost always better. Discuss more legal concepts, discuss more facts, make more arguments. One of the most common mistakes of trial lawyers is to carry this mind-set over into trials. At trial, *fewer* witnesses, fewer exhibits, and fewer arguments make for a better plaintiff's case. The same is true for criminal defense, when the defense attempts to persuade the jury of a particular story rather than just create doubt about the prosecution's story.

The problem of presenting too much of a case is so common there is a name for it: *overtrying the case.* It means you have brought too much evidence, made too many arguments, talked to the jury too long. This is one of the most common mistakes trial lawyers make.

This subject could fill a whole book, and it does: *Winning Jury Trials,* by Robert Klonoff and Paul Colby.[8] I will not attempt to summarize

---

8. Robert H. Klonoff and Paul L. Colby, *Winning Jury Trials: Trial Tactics and Sponsorship Strategy,* 2d ed. (LexisNexis, 2002).

this excellent book, but I strongly urge you to read it. It might pound home the point I will try to make in just a few pages. Experienced trial lawyers have known for years that too much evidence or argument can hurt a case. Many of the largest verdicts come from remarkably short trials. Multimillion-dollar verdicts can come from trials lasting less than a week.

To understand how too much evidence can hurt your case, let's go back to the basics. To win a case, you must present a story that is easy to understand, consistent, believable, and compelling. These qualities overlap, of course. A story that is inconsistent is usually not believable. A story hard to understand is usually not compelling. Let's look at these qualities one at a time and examine how too much evidence can undercut the effectiveness of your case.

## Keep Your Story Easy to Understand

Ultimately, we are trying to get the jury to *do something*. Inertia favors the defense in a civil case and the prosecution in a criminal case. Awarding money to someone goes against the grain in our present culture; so does finding a criminal defendant not guilty. The path of least resistance for the jurors is a small verdict or a defense verdict in a civil case and a guilty verdict in a criminal case. These are the jury's default positions as the trial begins.

If we want jurors to do something our culture conditions them to resist, they need to understand why they are doing it. To understand why they are doing it, they need to understand our story. The more complicated the story, the more resistance they have.

Think of your own experience when trying to learn something new, complicated, and not particularly interesting. Your first reaction is probably to just give up—"I don't need to know how to program the remote control anyway." You have this reaction, even if you would very much like to be able to program the remote control.

As you add witnesses, exhibits, and arguments to your case, the story almost always becomes more complicated. You also give the civil defense lawyers opportunities to make the case more complicated. Since complexity and confusion favor the defense, you can count on them to jump on these opportunities.

## Keep Your Story Consistent

Inconsistencies make a story harder to understand, less believable, and less compelling. That much is obvious. What is less obvious is that every new piece of evidence you introduce can create inconsistencies in your story. Let's use a simple fact pattern to illustrate this problem.

Your client is hit from behind while stopped at a traffic light. The driver who hit her comes up to her and asks if she is all right. Your client testifies that she told the driver, "I feel okay, but my neck got yanked." Two witnesses are on the sidewalk when this exchange occurs. The first witness tells you he heard your client say, "Okay, but my neck hurts." The second witness tells you he heard your client say, "Okay, but my back got yanked."

Suppose the defense claims your client simply said she was okay and not hurt immediately after the accident, and you want to introduce testimony to show that your client was immediately aware she might have been hurt. The differences between your client's version and the first witness's version are not significant enough to cause any problems.

Some lawyers might also have the second witness testify, out of a desire to hammer home that plaintiff was aware from the beginning she was hurt and her present claims are not later fabrications.

Now your story becomes inconsistent. Did she say "back" or "neck?" Did she say two different things right after the accident? Are the witnesses lying out of a desire to help plaintiff and unable to keep their stories straight?

Every time you call an additional witness to prove a point, you create a very real risk of inconsistencies. People at the same event focus on different things, remember things differently, and use different words to express the same ideas. The problem is even worse with experts. Two qualified experts will almost always disagree on certain points; and competent opponents will seize on this to make your case appear inconsistent. "The plaintiff's own hired experts can't even agree on these points…"

Even if two witnesses are consistent on the points that concern you, they may be inconsistent on other points. These inconsistencies may come out inadvertently on direct examination. They are even more likely to come out on cross-examination. A well-known cross-examination tactic is to question adverse witnesses on collateral matters, hoping to discover and capitalize on inconsistencies.

Suppose one witness says a passenger was in the plaintiff's car, and another witness says there wasn't. All of a sudden, the jury is wondering about your client's credibility, what was going on in the car, or why the passenger disappeared from the scene.

These sorts of inconsistencies can range from being merely distracting to destroying your case. Every additional witness or document increases the risk.

Documents, in fact, have a particularly pernicious way of creating inconsistencies. Let's keep using our simple car crash example to illustrate. It may be undisputed that your client went to the emergency room the day after the accident. After the ER exam, the ER doctor referred her to an orthopedist, who became her treating doctor.

Many plaintiff's lawyers will introduce the ER records just because they think they should or because they believe the records will make their case or the client's injuries look more substantial.

The problem is that many doctors are poor historians—especially about facts not material to medical diagnosis or treatment. So although your client testified that the accident happened on the way to the grocery store, the medical record might say, "Patient was on her way to pick up her children at school when she was hit from behind."

"So," the defense lawyer says, "why would she tell us one thing and her doctor something else?" Of course, counsel doesn't even need to say that; jurors are very likely to pick up on such inconsistencies on their own.

It should be obvious that the more complex the case, the more opportunities there are for inconsistencies to arise. This is yet another reason to keep your case as simple and straightforward as possible.

## Keep Your Story Believable

If the jury does not believe your version, your story, you lose. A simple story or explanation is almost always more believable than a complex one. This is why politicians gravitate toward slogans and sound bites.

Compare "We will fight the terrorists in Iraq, so we don't have to fight them here at home," with "The causes of terrorism are numerous and complex, requiring us to address cultural and economic forces that span the globe and are centuries old…" Regardless of your views on the Iraq war, the instant appeal of the first argument over the second should be obvious—to everyone except some lawyers.

Some lawyers have a natural affinity for complex stories, arguments, and explanations. Law school cultivates and encourages this affinity. For some types of law, this affinity may be an asset; for trial law it is deadly. If you cannot take complex facts and concepts and reduce them to direct, simple stories, you have no business trying cases.

Think of movies or television shows you have seen. How do stereotypical liars behave? Do they give a simple, direct explanation? Not usually. More often than not, particularly in comedies, they give long convoluted explanations and descriptions.

Remember, as a trial lawyer, you are laboring under an additional handicap when it comes to complex explanations. Our culture already conditions jurors to expect trial lawyers to try to obscure the truth by manipulating complex concepts and words—using double-talk. The jurors come to court believing you are the evasive slippery lawyer trying to lead them astray. The more complex and wordy your presentation, the less credible it is.

I cannot emphasize this point strongly enough. If anything is remotely close to a formula for effective trial advocacy, it is that the simpler the explanation or story, the more likely the jury is to believe it.

## Keep Your Story Compelling

Ultimately, all trial lawyers are looking for a way to make their case compelling. What is it that makes a jury want to act? A likable client? A rags-to-riches life story? A David and Goliath battle? An evil defendant? The question has no single answer. The essence of advocacy is discerning and presenting what is compelling about your client's case. Trial lawyers, social scientists, and jury consultants constantly grapple with this question—and will for centuries to come. I am not prepared to give you a framework or formula to make every case compelling.

I can, however, tell you how to suck whatever might be compelling out of your case—overtry it. Present three witnesses when one will do; present an expert witness on every conceivable issue; offer a thousand documents into evidence when you only need ten; make complicated, convoluted arguments; take two weeks to present a case that you could have presented in two days. I have seen it happen again and again; strong, compelling cases are lost under the weight of too much evidence.

I once watched an interview with a prominent movie director. Asked what characteristic set great directors apart from merely good directors, he replied that *great* directors are willing to edit out their favorite scene for the good of the movie. Trial lawyers need this same sense of discipline. *When in doubt, cut it out.*

# CHAPTER TWELVE

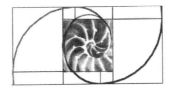

# Strategic Detachment: Don't React to Every Attack or Issue

e know we must fight for our clients. If our adversary does
**W** something improper, we object; if the judge shows signs of
wavering on an important issue, we push the judge hard. If we are
doing our duty, if we are not afraid, we never give an inch. *Wrong.*
Our job is more subtle, difficult, and artful than that.

Objections, timing issues, and working with the judge are all
closely related. They involve letting go of the idea that there is only
one way to fight for the client—by being aggressive and never yield-
ing an inch.

## Objections

Let's start with a basic truth that some lawyers can't seem to grasp: *Every
time you make an evidentiary objection in front of the jury, it costs you.*
You are announcing loud and clear to the jurors that the other side is
about to show them evidence that will hurt your case—and you want to
keep it from them. What does this do to your credibility? Interestingly,
it may not hurt your personal or professional credibility with the jurors,
but it may hurt your case's credibility. I say it *may* not hurt your own
credibility, but it certainly can. You show yourself to be the typical lawyer, trying to hide the truth so you can win.

Maybe the jurors will be more understanding. Some expect lawyers to make the best case on behalf of their client and respect a lawyer who fights to do so. They expect lawyers to object. If they otherwise like you, they may respect your willingness to fight hard to present a certain view of the truth to them—including hiding bad facts. Still, the message they receive is clear: this lawyer I like and respect thinks this evidence hurts the client's case. In effect, your own credibility is vouching for the importance of the point your opponent is making.

When you make an objection, you:

1. Immediately draw the jury's attention to the issue raised by the other side. Jurors who were merely drifting are now locked in on that point.

2. Announce to the jury that this evidence hurts your case.

That is bad enough, but the truth is that lawyers lose most evidentiary objections made in front of the jury. By *lose,* I mean your opponent eventually gets the same information (or remarkably similar information) presented to the jury in some other way.[9] You object on foundation grounds, and your opponent asks a few more questions to lay a foundation. You object on hearsay grounds, and your opponent asks different questions to show the judge the statement is not being offered for the truth of the matter asserted, but to explain what the witness did next.

If you win the objection, and the jurors never hear another word about the subject, they are still left to wonder what you kept from them—what you are trying to hide.

---

9. I am not talking here of the evidentiary objections made and resolved through motions *in limine* prior to trial.

Some will argue that good lawyers need to "make a record," so that if they lose the case, the chances will be greater on appeal. This argument has two responses, one for civil lawyers, and one for criminal lawyers.

Here is an exercise for civil lawyers. Find ten reported cases in which an appellate court reversed a defense verdict. That alone is hard enough. Our best chance is always in front of a jury. If we lose there, appellate courts are not inclined to help us. But you will eventually find ten cases. Read them carefully. How many involved a reversal based even in part on an evidentiary issue raised for the first time in front of the jury? I would bet none of them. Find one hundred cases in which an appellate court reversed a defense verdict. Again, how many of these reversals were based on evidentiary issues raised for the first time in front of a jury? Again, probably none. I am not saying it never happens, but the chances are about the same as being struck by lightning.

Because evidentiary rulings are discretionary, the admission of evidence against the plaintiff is almost never prejudicial enough, in the appellate court's eyes, to justify reversal. Unless the defense has clearly gone over the line in an obvious and extremely prejudicial way, all your objection accomplishes is a chipping away at the credibility of your case.

Yes, it is scary not to make objections. It's what we learned to do in law school. It's what real lawyers do. If we lose the case, we can be criticized for not objecting. (This might be a good time to reread Chapter Ten, on playing it safe.)

For criminal defense lawyers, the analysis is somewhat different. Unexpected prejudicial evidence is more likely to surprise you in the midst of trial. Jurors are more likely to forgive a criminal defense lawyer's objections. Appellate courts are somewhat more willing to reverse guilty verdicts on evidentiary grounds than they are civil defense verdicts. Still, most of the objections I see in criminal cases are about minor evidentiary issues that will never determine outcomes. Criminal defense lawyers need to be conscious that every objection creates a risk of loss of credibility with the jury. Is your objection worth it? The answer is often no.

This is not to say you shouldn't object to the admission of harmful evidence. Almost always, you will see it coming a mile away. Make your motion *in limine* before trial and get your ruling. If the judge rules against you, ask to have a continuing objection to this evidence at trial so you don't need to interrupt and slow things down. Most judges will give this to you. If you have not filed a motion *in limine* and you become aware of something harmful that may come in front of the jury, ask to take it up outside the jury's presence—usually at the beginning or end of the day. Again, most judges appreciate having evidentiary issues raised outside the jury's presence.

Sometimes you have no choice. Something very harmful that you did not anticipate comes up at trial. You need to stop it early, before it gets worse; you have no choice but to object. This can happen, but it should be rare.

Objections may be appropriate in a few other situations. One is if you are before one of the increasingly rare judges who allow "speaking objections." Most judges now require one-word or one-rule objections, such as "irrelevant" or "Evidence Rule 401." Any argument then takes place at the bench. A few judges still allow evidentiary argument in front of the jury. In that case, you can often eliminate any credibility loss from making an objection by letting the jury in on the basis for your objection. You might say, for example, "Objection, hearsay. The defense is not willing to bring Mr. Howard here to testify and instead is trying to have Mr. Wilson speak for him."

Another situation in which objections can be appropriate is when the defense is doing something highly improper and you *know* the judge will be displeased. If your opponent has violated an *in limine* order, for example, you may want to object immediately and let the judge's wrath rain down in front of the jury. The problem with even this approach, however, is that most judges have a high tolerance for civil defense and prosecutorial misbehavior. Only if the opposition has violated the judge's order repeatedly is a judge likely to show displeasure in front of the jury.

This is not a book about trial technique, so I will not attempt to catalog the various situations in which objections are appropriate. My point is simply that lawyers commonly hurt their cases by objecting too much. I suggest erring on the side of not objecting in front of the jury. Anytime you feel yourself automatically objecting, stop yourself. Anytime you find yourself thinking you must object, re-examine your assumptions.

One more common example emphasizes this point. Suppose a defense expert is on the stand, giving long, rambling, argumentative, and nonresponsive answers. You know the judge is displeased and will sustain your objections. Many lawyers tell me that in this situation they have no choice but to object. Why is that? Is the expert saying anything he couldn't eventually say anyway? Are you afraid he is going to mesmerize the jury? The jurors know he is hired to mesmerize them. The more it looks as if he is putting on a show, the better it is for you. Maybe he is hurting you, but your objections are not going to stop the pain. Trying to interrupt, disrupt, or limit him is not going to help you with the jury—it will just make you look afraid. Let him put on his show and then do your cross-examination.

The practice of not objecting can take great self-discipline. I once came close to blows with a co-counsel who vehemently disagreed with this approach. However, I can tell you that it works, for me and for others.

I sometimes go through a two- or three-week trial without making a single objection. Other times, I may make only one or two. Watch most successful trial lawyers with significant experience, and you will see the same thing. Something else can also happen when you use this approach. The judge, who is used to objections, starts to look over at you when your opponent is doing improper things. If you sit calmly, clearly disinclined to do anything, the judge may start objecting on your behalf. "That's irrelevant counsel. Move on." "I've already ruled on that, counsel."

Sometimes judges do this out of a sense of propriety—a sense of how trials should be run. Sometimes they do it to speed things along. I would say that in about half my trials, by the time we are three or four days into the case, the judge is objecting for me on at least some occasions. And aren't those the most effective objections of all?

## Timing Issues

You can divide timing issues into two categories: legal and factual. I wish to make the same point about each category: *Sometimes your arguments improve with time.* A common mistake of trial lawyers is to try to get all issues settled, settled right, and settled immediately. Many arguments and even cases are lost this way.

Let's take a legal example first. At the pretrial hearing, the judge rules against you on a defense motion *in limine* and excludes an important piece of evidence. You believe the judge does not fully understand the facts. Being a fearless lawyer who fights for your client, knowing you are legally and factually correct, you try to explain to the judge—politely, of course—where she has gone wrong.

The judge is in a hurry. (Aren't they all?) She has seven other motions to hear that morning. She has told you her ruling, and you are telling her she is wrong. Is this how the trial is going to go? Who's in charge here anyway? There is a good chance the judge will shut you down and dig even deeper into her position that she should exclude the evidence. Your fear is that once the judge starts going against you on an issue, she will be like a freight train you won't be able to stop. That is rarely the case.

What if you accept the judge's ruling and move on? Then, a day or two into the trial, when you have the judge's full attention, and one hopes her trust, you ask to go on record out of the presence of the jury. You say something like: "Your Honor, at the pretrial hearing you granted the defense motion to exclude the testimony of Mrs. Samuels. Since that ruling, we heard defense counsel in opening statement say, _____. We have also heard him cross-examine two witnesses, each time referring to _____. Given what has happened, I would ask permission to call Mrs. Samuels."

You may have made almost identical arguments at the pretrial hearing, but now the judge understands the trial better and the context of the evidence you seek to admit. Even more important, it is very likely that your opponent, emboldened by the *in limine* ruling and forgetting that *in limine* rulings are always tentative, may have given you new ammunition for your argument.

I am not saying you should never try to convince judges they are wrong when they first rule against you. Sometimes that is the right thing to do. But I frequently see lawyers desperately trying to change a judge's mind prematurely. It's as if they think they only have one chance to get a judge to rule their way, and a ruling against them becomes set in stone. This is not true of *in limine* rulings.[10] It is not true of most trial court rulings.[11]

Obviously, you don't want to keep arguing with the judge or without good reason revisit arguments you have lost. But with the ebb and flow of trial almost always gives you a second chance to persuade a judge you are right. The second chance may be a better opportunity to convince the judge than the first.

This is particularly true if you are on the right side of an issue. The converse is also true. If you are on the wrong side of an issue, your best bet is to push the judge hard to rule before the judge fully understands what is going on. That is one reason why civil defense lawyers are so aggressive in trying to get rulings in their favor at the pretrial stage. They know as time goes on their arguments will become less and less convincing.

Your factual points may also improve as the trial progresses. For example, in opening statement, the defense makes a powerful point to the jury: in the first six months after the accident, not a single treating doctor diagnosed concussion or brain injury in your client. You can tell that point is having a strong impact on the jury. But the defense has overlooked the fact that the first treating doctors used the Current Procedural Terminology (CPT) codes of 850.1, 310.2, and 310.8, indicating brief loss of consciousness, postconcussion syndrome, and brain injury.

---

10. *See People v. Yarbrough,* 227 Cal. App. 3d 1650, 1655, 278 Cal. Rptr. 703, 705–06 (Cal. App. 1991) (court may modify orders at any time); *Rufo v. Simpson,* 86 Cal. App. 4th 573, 608, 103 Cal. Rptr. 2d 492, 516 (Cal. App. 2001) ("A ruling on a pretrial motion *in limine* is necessarily tentative because subsequent evidentiary development may change the context"); *Zimmerman v. Skakman,* 204 Ariz. 231, 62 P.3d 976, 981 (App. 2003) (At the trial court level, the law of the case doctrine "does not prevent a judge from reconsidering nonfinal rulings, '[n]or does it prevent a different judge, sitting on the same case, from reconsidering the first judge's prior, nonfinal rulings'").

11. It is well settled that "district court orders are subject to revision at any time prior to the entry of judgment adjudicating all of the claims." *Williamson v. UNUM Life Ins. Co. of America,* 160 F.3d 1247, 1251 (9th Cir. Cal. 1998); *Industrial Bldg. Materials, Inc. v. Interchemical Corp.,* 437 F.2d 1336, 1345 (9th Cir. Cal. 1970); *See United States v. Desert Gold Mining Co.,* 433 F.2d 713, 715 (9th Cir., 1970). *See also Wright & Miller,* 10 Fed. Prac. & Proc. Civ. 3d § 2660.

One response is to immediately call a witness who can explain CPT codes to the jury and point out that the doctors did in fact diagnose concussion and brain injury. This has the benefits of immediately putting your opponent's argument to rest, hurting the opponent's credibility, and enhancing your own. This will often be the best thing to do.

Another alternative is to let your opponent keep building the defense on this faulty pillar. Let your opponent keep referring to the "fact" that no treating doctor diagnosed concussion or brain injury. Once that fact becomes totally identified with the strength of the defense case—becomes synonymous with the defense case—then you prove it false. Part of the skill in trying cases is learning to use timing to your best advantage. Trials are full of second and third chances to make points, refute arguments, and reshape the judge's and jurors' opinions. Many lawyers forget this.

If you are aware that delayed gratification is sometimes the best approach, you will be calmer when things go against you at trial. You will not feel as compelled to react immediately. This is a good thing. Often, the piece of evidence that hurt so badly at 11:00 A.M. seems inconsequential at 2:00 P.M. Often, no reaction is the best reaction.

## Work with the Judge

Appearing before the judge for a pretrial conference or for the first day of trial is a little like going on a first date. You may have some familiarity with the other person, but you are now entering into a new phase of your relationship. What does this person expect of me? Will she like me? Will I be comfortable with her? Will she be comfortable with me? *Can I feel safe with her? Can I trust her?*

Judges have to be on guard. The world is full of people trying to manipulate and take advantage of them. You want the judge's trust and respect; you can't take it, any more than you can take trust and respect from anyone else.

An entire book could be written about lawyers' relationships with judges, and one probably will be some day. In the meantime, I would like to focus on two aspects of these relationships: timing and flexibility.

On a first date, most men would not say to the woman across the table, "I hope to order our meal, eat our meal, and then take you back to my apartment for hot, passionate sex that will last for hours." Yet lawyers do the equivalent of that with judges every day. Before the judge fully understands the case, before he has any level of comfort with the lawyer, the lawyer pushes the judge hard, trying to get every possible advantage. The judge is being rushed, and he knows it. He does not want to make a mistake. He may have been inclined to rule in the lawyer's favor, just as your date may have been inclined to go to your apartment, but the very act of pushing and rushing reduces your chances.

Many issues raised pretrial can wait for resolution until the trial is well under way. The more clearly you are entitled to win on an issue, the more likely it can wait for later resolution. Imagine going to the pretrial hearing and saying something like this to the judge: "Your Honor, we have made six *in limine* motions, and the defense has made five. As far as I can tell, only two of our motions and three of the defense motions need to be resolved before jury selection and opening statements."

All judges are different. Some will say they want to address all the motions then and there. Others will be relieved that they can postpone some of the decision making until they are better prepared. All will appreciate your attempt to guide them in a fair and evenhanded manner.

Let's turn to the related issue of flexibility. Suppose you went even further in your comments to the judge, and said something like: "Your Honor, we have made six *in limine* motions. Upon further reflection, I believe we can withdraw motions three and four. Of the remaining four motions, you only need to resolve one and two before jury selection and opening statements."

In preparing for trial, most lawyers unleash a barrage of motions *in limine* covering every issue they can think of at the time. Once the motions are filed and additional trial preparation takes place, some of the *in limine* motions invariably seem less meritorious, less important, or even unnecessary.

I have heard various arguments for *not* withdrawing such motions. Some lawyers say that this is a way of negotiating with the judge. The judge will rule against them on these motions, and then go their way on the more critical ones. Or, they argue, withdrawing the motions will make them look weak.

It is true that some judges seem to keep score—"one ruling for you, one ruling for them"—but these judges are a minority. Most judges try to focus on the substance and try to get the rulings right. One thing they are constantly judging is the messenger—you. If you make three frivolous motions, it will hurt you when the judge turns to your motion that is meritorious, but a close legal call.

As for looking weak, this argument is not only exactly wrong; it also reveals an attitude that can easily get you into trouble. What could look stronger than saying, in effect, "I don't need to bother the court with these issues"? You are letting the judge see that your case is strong and you are smart enough to see it.

When I began practicing law, young lawyers were told they needed to be strong in the courtroom, to take control, to be the leader. Many interpreted this to mean they needed to fight the judge for control, prove they were not awed by the judge's power, and prove they were willing to push back. Imagine going on a date or entering into a marriage and receiving the advice that you must take control and be the leader. How successful do you think the relationship would be if you followed the advice?

Your goal should be to work *with* the judge. If judges think you are trying to take control or prove something, they'll be trying to prove something back. And of course, they have the last word. If they sense that you believe part of your job is to try to make their job easier (it is) and to try to make sure they get things legally right (it is), they will start working *with* you, as they should.

I am not suggesting you act like a milquetoast wimp or that you not be firm with a judge when that is called for. But don't *start* your relationship with a judge by pushing, rushing, or trying to prove anything other than that you are a competent lawyer who can be trusted.

# CHAPTER THIRTEEN

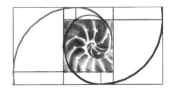

# Your Lawyer Status Carries No Weight with the Jury

We work hard to get into law school, we work hard to get through law school, and we work hard to pass the bar exam. When clients come to see us, they hang on our every word. So do our relatives when they ask us legal questions around the kitchen table.

Here is a sad truth: although our status as lawyers may enhance our credibility when talking with clients, family, and friends, *it hurts our credibility when talking with jurors.* In today's climate, this seems like an obvious observation. It perplexes me that more lawyers don't understand it and see the implications.

Put yourself in the juror's shoes. This lawyer stands in front of you in the courtroom. He may have a lot more education than you, but you don't really know what that education consisted of. You're pretty sure lawyers are trained how to fool people, people like you. You've heard the lawyer jokes. You've seen lawyers on television lying and cheating to win. You've seen lawyers' advertisements. This is all about the money. This lawyer is going to try to fool you so he can make a lot of money. He's probably good at it. He knows things about the case you don't know. He knows things about the law you don't know. He knows how to use words and phony emotions to fool people, people like you.

Do you think because jurors are not saying this to your face, they don't think it?

No, not every juror feels this way about lawyers. But it is the ones who *do* feel this way that you have to worry about—first, because their feelings are so strong, and second, because they are in the majority. How many people do you think get a warm, fuzzy feeling when they hear the word *lawyer?*

Here is a related point, before we move on to the implications of these attitudes: *Jurors don't care about you.* You are simply not that interesting to the juror. Although to you it appears you are center stage in a high drama starring yourself, to the juror you have a bit part in a tedious drama starring the *juror.*

What are the implications of these juror attitudes? For one thing, the jurors don't care about your personal history or demographics. Attempts to bond with them by talking about your children, your dog, or your college are likely to be met with suspicion. (Not openly, of course.) Especially during *voir dire,* they are likely to think this is just part of your act to manipulate them. Isn't it? What does your dog or your college have to do with the case? Some lawyers are so charming and personable they can talk about their own history without looking manipulative, but for the rest of us this is a dangerous approach.

This point warrants an important qualification. It is perfectly acceptable to bring up personal issues as a way to make it easier for jurors to talk about their own personal issues. If, for example, it is necessary to question a juror about his divorce, you might say something like: "Mr. Thompson, when I was just two months past my own divorce, I don't think I could have talked about it in front of a group of people. Would you prefer we talk about this privately in the judge's office?" Or perhaps: "I was once burglarized, and don't think I could ever again make a good juror in a burglary case. Do you think the fact that you were the victim of shoplifting could affect you the same way?"

You are giving the juror permission to have a problem or an issue by disclosing that you have (or have had) a similar issue. The jurors rightly understand you are trying to make things easier for them, rather than trying to manipulate them.

Similarly, Gerry Spence recommends that you talk with the jury panel about the issues in the case that scare you; this is not only permissible, but advisable. For example, "I'm afraid that because my client speaks only Spanish, some people may hold that against him."

Note that in these examples, although you are talking about matters personal to you, those matters relate directly to the case. The jurors understand how they relate to the case and why you must talk of them.

Jurors do not care about your opinions. They know you are a hired gun. When you say, "The defendant was outrageously reckless," or "This corporation only cared about profits," you are not convincing at all. Much better to say, "The traffic light had been red for thirty seconds when defendant ran through it at fifty miles per hour," or "In a memo dated December 12, 2002, the head of the engineering department wrote that $5 million could be saved by not installing this safety device."

In other words, keep your opinions and editorial comments to yourself—particularly in *voir dire* and opening statement. By the end of the trial, the jurors may be more interested in hearing your opinions, but probably not. They want the facts.

This is not all bad news. If, like me, you are naturally shy and self-conscious, this can be very liberating. If the jurors don't care about you, you're free to relax and present the facts. Knowing the focus is *not* on you enables you to focus on your case and your material; you don't need to be so self-conscious. You are not that important to them, so why worry so much about every word and body gesture?

The jurors also don't care about your emotions—how you feel about the case. If it appears you don't believe in your case, that can be fatal, for obvious reasons. But the fact that you are angry or sad or indignant will not carry your case very far with the jury.

If emotions from a plaintiff's lawyer or criminal defense lawyer can look manipulative, the effect can be compounded by a concept called "induced emotion." The concept of induced emotion posits that in any situation, a certain amount of emotion feels appropriate. If two people are in a situation, the amount of emotion one expresses tends to reduce the amount the other feels or expresses. This is best explained with an example.

Suppose you and I are at a restaurant. Our waiter is insolent and rude. It seems as though he is intentionally trying to offend us. Assume that emotion can be measured, and that the amount of anger each of us should experience in this situation is "five," bringing our total anger to "ten." If I act unconcerned about the waiter's behavior, you start to experience more and more anger. My lack of anger induces you to not only experience your own anger, but also mine. You may look as though you are overreacting by expressing anger at a level ten when level five is really more appropriate.

We all know married couples who act like this. One of them experiences certain emotions for both of them. The wife stays calm in the restaurant with the rude waiter, and the husband overreacts.

This principle can work in the other direction as well. Faced with the rude waiter, I immediately go to an anger level of ten. This leaves no room for your anger, so you remain calm. If I go to an anger level of fifteen, you get extremely calm; you push back emotionally, making the point, directly or indirectly, that my level of anger is not appropriate.

The same thing happens in the courtroom. If you are emotional in opening statement, venting your anger at the defendant, you leave little room for the jurors' anger. They may even push back, finding ways to view your anger as inappropriate. One friend of mine expresses this concept by saying, "You should never let your emotions get out ahead of the jurors'." Gerry Spence expresses a similar concept, saying you should not destroy a witness until the jury wants that witness destroyed.

Emotions can be contagious, but only when they come from an emotionally credible source.[12] You are not a credible source at the beginning of the trial. That you are angry, sad, or indignant counts for nothing with the jury. Worse, it can hurt your case because the jurors view you as manipulative or as overreacting. Either will cause them to emotionally retreat from your case. Maybe by the end of the trial you will be a credible source of emotion. Even then, though, make sure you leave room for jurors to have their own emotions.

If the jurors don't care about your personal history, opinions, or emotions, what do they care about? That's simple if you think about what the trial process is asking of them, from their point of view. They are being asked to make an important, serious decision about a subject that—at least at first—they know nothing about. They are totally dependent on just three sources of information: you, your opponent, and the judge.

*The jurors care whether you are a reliable source of information.* They know you are an advocate, but are you a fair, evenhanded advocate? Will you give them facts they can rely on or facts out of context? Will you bring them honest witnesses or people trying to

12. Daniel Goleman, *Social Intelligence* (Bantam Books, 2006).

shade the truth? Will you show them the whole document or just the parts that favor your side? Will you try to force emotions on them they don't yet feel?

The jurors will watch you like a hawk, judging you. Are you prepared? Are you accurate? Do you have common sense? Are you able to tell the difference between the important and unimportant or do you waste their time?

Finally, most jurors believe that, in a trial, one side deserves to win and one side deserves to lose and the lawyers know which is which. The lawyer who knows she deserves to lose is putting on a show, trying to fool them. Which lawyer is putting on a show? They are always watching for signs of phoniness.

# CHAPTER FOURTEEN

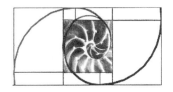

# Forget About Looking Good

Do you want the jurors leaving the courthouse thinking you are the smartest lawyer in the county? The nicest? The most charming? The most aggressive? Or do you want to win? Many lawyers, without even thinking about it, choose impressing the jury over winning.

We are all social creatures. It is natural to want our audience, the jurors, to think well of us. Our egos crave attention and approval. This natural desire trips up many trial lawyers on their way to a verdict. Let's look at just a few of the ways the need to look good can manifest itself at trial. See if you recognize yourself.[13]

## Acting Like an Actor

We all grew up watching lawyers on television and in the movies, so it is easy to believe that looking good to the jury means behaving like the actors we have seen on the small and large screens. We buy the clothes and don an attitude of exaggerated self-confidence. We throw big legal words around and do everything we can to look cool, sophisticated, and in control.

---

13. By the way, the points in this chapter are just as applicable to how the judge will perceive you as they are to how the jurors will perceive you. Judges watch for the same human clues and make the same human judgments as jurors.

Whether we intend to or not, our message to the jury is, "I am different from you; I am a Lawyer." The message is also, "I am better than you—because I am a Lawyer." How do you think jurors receive that message?

Acting like a television lawyer can also take the form of feigning emotions you don't feel. While actually feeling anxiety or fear, you may be displaying moral outrage, sadness, or grief. I can't make this point often enough: jurors are hypersensitive to phony emotions. They can see right through the most gifted actor. They will see through your act and punish you for it.

## Being Aggressive and Controlling

We discussed the issues of aggressiveness and control in Chapter Twelve, but they are worth revisiting. Many young lawyers are told to take control of the courtroom and show the judge they won't back down; after all, the jury respects lawyers willing to fight hard for their clients.

There is more than a grain of truth in each of these slogans—which is what makes them so dangerous. There are times to take control of the courtroom—they occur at maybe two or three points in the course of a trial. You may need to show a judge that you won't back down—maybe once every two or three trials. Jurors *do* respect a lawyer willing to fight hard for the client. But if you are argumentative and disagreeable, they won't like you at all. If you seem more interested in fighting than in getting at the truth, you will lose their respect, not gain it.

An additional problem with an excessive display of aggression or control is that, once again, you will tend to look like a performer rather than a truth seeker. Do I need to tell you that is not good?

## Sucking Up to the Jury

Absolutely nothing is worse in the courtroom than an obsequious lawyer. Yet we want so badly for the jury to like us that this tendency is hard to resist. The jurors spot exaggerated politeness or solicitude as quickly as fear-driven phoniness—often, they are the same thing.

I don't believe the lawyers who engage in this conduct do it consciously. If you are doing it, you probably won't recognize yourself. All I can tell you is that jurors want a straight-talking, honest, caring teacher. They don't want someone sucking up to them.

## Refusing to Admit Mistakes

If mistakes are inevitable and perfection is unattainable, then you will make mistakes in trial. Judges and jurors will see them. Why hide them or pretend they aren't there? Admit your mistake, as you would in any other real-life situation (you would, wouldn't you?), and move on.

## Joking and Being Friendly with Your Opponent

You are in court because something *serious* is happening. The government is trying to send your client to jail, or your client was injured, her life has been altered, and you are asking for justice. Your opponent represents the government, which is trying to send your client to jail, or the defendant who hurt your client and is now trying to avoid responsibility.

Many trial lawyers will be friendly or joke with their opponent because they believe this shows they are professionals, comfortable in the courtroom, and at ease with others in the workplace. When you are friendly or overly casual with your opponent where the jurors can see, you simultaneously communicate two messages.

1. Neither this case nor what my opponent is trying to do to my client is that important.

2. This is just a game or business as usual for the lawyers.

These messages can undermine or even kill your case. Experienced prosecutors and civil defense attorneys know this. They will work hard to engage you in friendly discussions where the jury can observe how well you get along. They will try particularly hard if you are a young lawyer. Impassively rebuff their advances. Say, "We need to talk about this later," and turn away. Or say, "We need to go to the conference room to talk about this." The more facile ones will make jokes during trial proceedings, trying to draw you into the banter. Smile politely at the jokes, but don't take the bait. If you don't take the case seriously, why should the jurors?

I am of course not suggesting that you be rude or unprofessional. But don't in any way convey that the case is anything but deadly serious to you. Better that you be thought humorless than that your case be thought frivolous.

## Trying to Hide Your True Self

This list of "looking good" behaviors is not exhaustive. We all have our own ways of trying to look good to the jury. What they all have in common is an effort to hide our true selves from the jury. We are afraid we will look weak, afraid, awkward, or stupid, so we adopt a behavior or style in the courtroom that is different from who we really are.

As if this constructed personality can save us.

As if the jury won't see through it.

Here is an unalterable truth of trial practice: *In the courtroom, you cannot be anyone other than who you are.* First, let's talk about the reality of this statement and then the way this truth affects juror perception.

If you are trying your first case, but acting smooth and sophisticated, the truth is that you *are* an inexperienced lawyer trying to act smooth and sophisticated. If you are a naturally shy or quiet person, but trying to act like a high-spirited extrovert, the truth is that you *are* a shy person trying to force yourself to act differently. Whether you like it or not, *you will always be who you are in the courtroom.* You can't escape yourself. The more you try, the more you hurt yourself in the jury's eyes.

If at bottom you are an inconsiderate person trying to cover up with exaggerated politeness and solicitude, the jury will know it in a few hours—probably sooner. If you are afraid, but try to cover up with aggression or exaggerated self-confidence, the jurors will know you are covering something up. Maybe they won't know you are hiding fear, but they will know you are not being authentic with them.

*Authentic* has become an overused word in trial advocacy seminars these days, but it is a good word. It is the opposite of *fake* or *phony.*

When you try to hide yourself from the jury, you create distrust. The jurors know immediately that you are hiding something. They may never figure out what you are hiding, but it doesn't matter; you have given them reason to distrust you. This leads us to another essential courtroom truth: *The greater the gap between how you act in the courtroom and who you are in the rest of your life, the greater your problems in court.* The corollary is: *The closer you are to your true self in the courtroom, the better you will do.*

Experienced trial lawyers have been preaching this truth at CLE seminars for decades. If you get to know successful trial lawyers, you can see this firsthand. Watch them in the courtroom; watch them interacting with friends and family. You will see very little difference in the personality on display, no matter what the setting.

What if you have a nasty, unlikable true self? First, you might want to work on that. Saying, "That's just the way I am," may make you feel better, but why exactly are you that way? If you are displaying traits and behaviors inappropriate for the situation, you have issues. They will not go away. They will not help you in the courtroom. They are probably not helping in the rest of your life. If you want to be a success in the courtroom, you had better light a candle, or you will be cursing the darkness for a long time.

Second, if you have characteristics you think may be off-putting to the jurors, don't pretend they're not there. You might say to the jury in *voir dire,* "My friends say I talk too fast, and I think that's probably true. I am trying to work on that, but there's probably a good chance I will get going a mile a minute before this trial is over. I'm hoping you won't hold that against my client, Mrs. Morgan." If you're really brave, say, "My wife says when I get stressed out, I get arrogant and overbearing. I don't mean to be that way, but since she's pointed it out, I can see it in myself sometimes in the courtroom. I'm hoping you won't hold that against my client, Mrs. Morgan."

If you confess your flaws, they lose much of their power to hurt you in the courtroom. All you need is the courage to identify your flaws and then confess them. In the end, it may be the lack of courage that stands between you and trial success—the courage to know yourself and not hide yourself from the jury. No matter how hard it is, no matter how awkward it feels, being real is the only way to "look good" to the jury.

# CHAPTER FIFTEEN

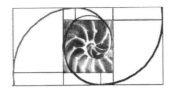

# Don't Try to Fool the Jury

Let me say what I don't think any other trial advocacy author has ever said in print. We *can* fool the jury.

For example, jurors may think our client is more likable than he or she really is. Or maybe we can minimize or maximize the degree of hostility between a party and a witness. By the way we ask questions and emphasize evidence, by the way we direct the spotlight, we can create an impression that deviates from the literal truth. This is a slippery issue, because there often is no literal truth. Our client may feel he has a warm and loving relationship with his sister, and his sister may have a totally different view. That one of these "truths" prevails with the jury does not mean the jury has been fooled—but it may.

It is also possible to fool the jury on larger issues and on issues that are more objective. Artful lawyering may completely fool the jury and result in a verdict inconsistent with the truth.

Knowing this, some lawyers feel it makes sense to try to disguise elements of the truth from the jury. The problem with this (putting aside moral and ethical issues) is that it is extremely risky behavior. The more important the issue, the less likely the jury will be fooled.

As a group, jurors are smart and perceptive. They take their work seriously. They will immediately spot the things about your case that keep you awake nights. If you cannot get these things excluded through motions *in limine,* you had better come clean about them at once. Trying to hide them is like playing Russian roulette with five bullets in the cylinder.

As we mature in our personal lives, we learn that no matter how hard it is to do, telling the truth is ultimately the less difficult, less risky course to follow. The same is absolutely true in the courtroom. I cannot honestly tell you that you will never be able to fool a jury. I *can* honestly tell you that you will *almost never* get away with it.

Gerry Spence recommends that you make a list of everything you are afraid of about your case and talk to the jury about it in *voir dire*. If you are not allowed *voir dire* in your jurisdiction, have the judge question jurors about these issues, and then *you* talk about them in opening. Like much good advice, this is simple, but difficult to follow.

But if you can bring these issues out in the open, they lose at least some of their power, and you increase your credibility. *Trying to hide the issues that scare you almost always leads to disaster.*

# CHAPTER SIXTEEN

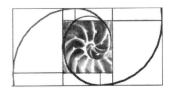

# Don't Assume the Jury Will Respond to Your Favorite Arguments

*One forgets the extent to which aesthetic standards are pro-
jections of one's own personality, defensive armor, or wishful
thinking about the world.*

—JOHN GARDNER, *On Becoming a Novelist*

I have never met you, but I would be willing to bet you are a nerd.
That you wanted to go to law school, did go to law school, and
passed the bar exam sets you apart from the general population. To
make matters worse, chances are you spend most of your time with
people like yourself.

Notice I am *not* saying you are smarter or morally superior to
anyone else. You simply tend to approach the world and solve problems in a particular way—a way that differs from how most people
approach the world and solve problems.

Many lawyers assume jurors view the world the way lawyers
do. Worse, they assume the jurors have an inferior way of viewing
the world and that, once exposed to the lawyer's more enlightened
view, they will easily give up their own.

If I am on vacation with my family in New York City and I want
to visit the Metropolitan Museum of Art, I will use different arguments

to convince each family member this is a good use of our time. I may tell my wife there is a display of French impressionist paintings. I may tell my daughter there is an exhibit of dresses worn by the First Ladies of our country. I may tell my son there is a large exhibit with more swords and armor than he has ever seen. All these things may be true, but they have nothing to do with my desire to see the Egyptian exhibit. But they *are* true. It is not manipulative or dishonest to use these arguments. Using these arguments shows that I understand my audience and respect them enough to believe they are entitled to their own preferences and values.

We are all different, aren't we? I don't know how trial lawyers can forget that, but they do. They give arguments centered on the values and perspective of the speaker (themselves), instead of their audience (the jurors). An example is a real estate agent my wife and I once had. We told him the type of house we were interested in, but he couldn't hear us. He kept showing us houses *he* was enthusiastic about. He was genuine and enthusiastic, but totally missed the mark. He could never find us a house, because he couldn't look beyond his own perspective.

I once tried a case in Arizona on behalf of a Mexican woman who had been in the country legally for thirty years. She spoke no English. To me, this was an inconvenience, but not a significant fact. My friends and co-counsel in Arizona warned me that some people in Arizona had strong feelings about those who came to the United States and did not learn English. I was oblivious to this. When they told me, I quickly discounted it. Yet focus groups confirmed it, as did discussions during *voir dire*.

I simply couldn't understand why there should be any hard feelings against someone in the country legally, who worked hard, followed the laws, and paid taxes. I couldn't see beyond my own point of view until it practically hit me in the face.

How do you get beyond your own perspective to discover arguments that might appeal to others? Keep an open mind. Be alert to other ways of viewing the facts and arguments. Broaden your circle of friends and acquaintances. Make a point of talking with people you ordinarily would not talk to. Watch television shows and movies you ordinarily would not watch. Read social science and psychological literature to develop a better understanding of how people think and make decisions. Use formal or informal focus groups, and talk to the jurors in *voir dire*. Correction: *listen* to the jurors in *voir dire*. Be quiet, and give them the opportunity to tell you what they think and feel.

A lawyer I know tries cases in a conservative area of Oklahoma. In this jurisdiction, arguing that the defendant was negligent in causing a traffic accident is a tough sell. The strong predisposition of jurors is that stuff happens, everyone makes mistakes, "There but for the grace of God go I," and the plaintiff should have been more careful. After attending a seminar on juror attitudes, he learned that conservative jurors place a high value on contractual obligations. These jurors embrace the "sanctity of contract" with an almost religious fervor. In his next personal injury case, he reframed a traditional negligence case to address the jurors' values. He said something like:

> *When we get our driver's license from the state, we are entering into a contract with the State of Oklahoma and all other drivers who are legally on the road. The laws of the state are the contract we all agree to follow. Among other things, all of us agree to yield when the state puts a yield sign up. A year and a half ago, at the corner of Elm and Shuster, Mr. Simpson broke that contract.*

His cross-examination followed up on this theme:

**Q:** When you got your driver's license, you were promising to follow the laws of this state?

**Q:** This was a promise made to the state?

**Q:** This was a promise made to all other drivers?

**Q:** You knew other drivers were promising the same thing to you?

**Q:** It is part of what made you feel safe on the road—the promises of these other drivers to follow the laws?

I don't know about you, but I think that is one of the most creative examples of advocacy I have ever heard. He won the case and several others that followed. Everyone makes mistakes, but if you break a contract—even by mistake—you have to pay.

This lawyer zeroed in on his audience's values. He didn't change the facts, just the lens through which his audience viewed them—a lens his audience valued. He had enough respect for the audience to make an argument—an honest argument—that would appeal to them. You should do the same. Present an audience-centered case.

# CHAPTER SEVENTEEN

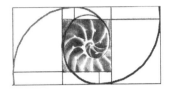

# The Limits of Logic and Sympathy

*The opposite of love is not hate, but the relentless pursuit of the rational mind.*

—JOSH KARTON, ACTOR, WRITER, "LAWYER WHISPERER" AND
TRIAL CONSULTANT, PURPORTING TO QUOTE DOSTOYEVSKY

Over and over again, I see lawyers convinced they will win because they have an airtight, logical case. The classic example of this is the case in which a child is suing a parent for negligence of some sort—usually driving a car improperly. Such claims are prohibited in many states, but where they are allowed the child's guardian (sometimes the other parent) usually brings them against the negligent parent.

The liability facts may be overwhelming. Let's say the father was drunk and crossed the center line, causing a collision. The damages may be clear. Let's say the five-year-old daughter is now a paraplegic. Logically, this is an airtight, open-and-shut, slam-dunk case. In reality, it's an extraordinarily difficult case.

No one (except maybe plaintiff's lawyers) likes the idea of children suing parents. This is true even if the jurors know or suspect insurance is involved. The thought that a family could get rich because the father got drunk and caused a crash repulses most jurors. They will find any way they can to render a defense verdict.

Similar situations arise with police excessive force cases. No matter how clear it is that a police officer overreacted and used excessive force, in some parts of the country such cases are almost impossible to win. Jurors in those venues are pretty much convinced that too many people survive the arrest process. A few miles away, in another county, the same case may be almost impossible to lose. The legal merits of the case have little to do with its strength.

In short, although it is always nice to have compelling legal logic on your side, having completely correct logic does not assure you victory—or even of having a strong case. Repeatedly, I see lawyers blinded by the logic of their case, unable to see how difficult it really is.

Lawyers can also be blinded by the sympathy they feel—and think the jury will feel—for their client. There may have been a time in the past when sympathy for a plaintiff was enough to guarantee success at trial. If there ever was such a time, it is long gone. Sympathy is one of the weakest emotions and the one least likely to motivate a jury. This is not to say that jurors can't feel sympathy. I have seen jurors with tears in their eyes return defense verdicts that guaranteed an injured plaintiff would live out the rest of her life in poverty.

Think again of our paraplegic five-year-old suing her father. The jurors will feel enormous sympathy for her, but are still likely to return a verdict against her.

If logic won't win your case, and sympathy won't win your case, what *will* win your case? Something else. I don't want to beg the question, but let me emphasize that if you think logic or sympathy will do it for you, you will stop looking for those things that truly motivate jurors.

Think of the lawyer in Oklahoma arguing personal injury traffic cases as contract cases. He didn't argue the logic of the defendant's negligence, and he didn't argue sympathy for the client. Had he relied on those, they would have blinded him to the real key to success—the sanctity of contract.

One of the best trial lawyers I know is Don Bauermeister in Anchorage, Alaska. Don makes the point that, ultimately, a jury verdict is a reflection of how the jurors see the world or would like the world to be. The Oklahoma lawyer, Don would say, is in effect asking the jurors if they want to live in a world where contracts can be violated without consequence. Conversely, Don would say, jurors do not want to live in a world where a drunken father can make his family rich by injuring his child in an auto accident. That is why suits by children against parents are so difficult.

Jurors want to live in a world that has hope, where people who break the rules are punished, where hard work is rewarded, where contracts are honored, where no one gets something for nothing. Plenty of books can help you better understand values that appeal to jurors. You can also learn about juror values by making a point to talk to a wide variety of people. If you don't let your case's logic or sympathy get in the way, you will have a better chance of seeing your case's value-centered core.

# CHAPTER EIGHTEEN

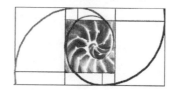

# Don't Gorge on Experts and Starve for Lay Witnesses

It is tempting to try to shore up a weak part of your case with expert testimony. The more insecure you are, the more likely you are to include too many experts in your case. With too many experts, you risk overtrying your case (see Chapter Eleven), losing momentum at trial, and going broke.

As you add more experts to your presentation, you also add to the potential—almost the certitude—that your experts will disagree about *something,* large or small. Do I need to tell you how your opponent will capitalize on the smallest disagreements between your experts? Maybe I do.

You will hear arguments that the inconsistencies show your experts are incompetent or perhaps simply trained prostitutes, with no allegiance to the truth. You will hear that if your highly trained experts cannot agree on even the small points, how could this ordinary defendant be expected to meet the vague and unreasonable standard the plaintiff is attempting to impose? Don't fool yourself. No matter how small the discrepancy between the opinions of your experts—even on immaterial matters—the opposition will blow it up to monumental size and make you highly uncomfortable.

Just as important, using too many experts may cause you to overlook the power of lay witnesses. Jurors know that lawyers can hire an expert to say anything. They are almost as distrustful of paid experts as they are of lawyers. Interestingly, they are much less distrustful of family, friends, and coworkers, if those witnesses are honest and matter-of-fact, don't exaggerate, and don't try to play on the jurors' emotions.

Lay witnesses are the most underutilized weapon in the trial lawyer's arsenal. I feel so strongly about the value of lay testimony that it was a major theme in my last book.[14] That book discusses in detail the use of lay witnesses and how to work with them to undermine defense experts. Here it is enough to say that a lack of attention to finding and working with lay witnesses is a major failing of many otherwise excellent trial lawyers.

To find lay witnesses, you have to work with *people*. I think that is why many trial lawyers neglect them. You have to knock on doors and talk to people who may have witnessed the accident. You have to work with your client and your client's family and friends. In short, you have to get on the phone or out of your office—or have someone else do it for you.

---

14. Rick Friedman, *Polarizing the Case: Exposing and Defeating the Malingering Myth* (Trial Guides, 2007).

# CHAPTER NINETEEN

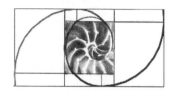

# Spend More Time with Witnesses and Clients

Once you find lay witnesses, you have to talk to them—sometimes for twenty minutes, sometimes for hours. That is the only way to determine the ones you should call for trial—and what you should ask them. Once you have decided who to call, you need to spend more time helping them prepare for deposition and trial.

Spending more time with witnesses—including clients—is probably the single most important thing *any* trial lawyer can do to improve his or her performance in the courtroom. Yet it is difficult. Everything about our practices conspires to keep us from spending the time we need with our witnesses. As a result, almost every lawyer is deficient in this area.

If we don't respond to discovery requests in time, the opposing counsel punishes us. If we don't respond to motions or pretrial deadlines on time, the judge punishes us. If we don't appear for status conferences or oral arguments, the judge punishes us again. If we don't respond to our employees' concerns in a timely manner, they punish us. If we don't pay our bills on time, our creditors punish us.

If we fail to spend the time we need with witnesses, nobody punishes us—at least not directly. When we have no one breathing down our necks to interview witnesses, it is easy to put this task low on the list of priorities. Yet when we step into the courtroom, the witnesses—and our knowledge of what they can say—are our primary weapons.

At the most basic level, a trial is a series of witnesses sitting in a chair, saying, "This is what I saw," "This is what I heard," or "This is what I did." These are the building blocks of the coherent story and argument you are trying to put together. These witnesses should be the center of your trial lawyer universe. Instead, the faxes, e-mails, motions *in limine,* phone calls, and broken copiers become the center of your universe, and the witnesses become afterthoughts.

As I write this, I am waiting for a verdict in a wrongful death case. Earlier today, I had dinner with my clients. As we discussed issues in the trial, they told me things I had not heard before—things that would have been helpful to our case. The jury never heard these things because I did not spend enough time with my clients; I did not ask them the right questions.

Atlanta trial lawyer Don Keenan says he makes it a point to spend at least one night as a guest in his client's home. He says he learns important things he never would otherwise: details of his clients' lives, how their injuries have affected the various family members, what makes his clients "tick." It is no coincidence Don is regarded as one of the finest trial lawyers in America—with a long string of phenomenal verdicts to prove it. If he is willing to go sleep in a shack and hang around in his bathrobe drinking coffee with his clients, shouldn't you at least pick up the phone and meet some witnesses at a restaurant? Better yet, go to their houses or offices?

Our job in the courtroom is difficult enough as it is. We cannot afford to give away points. Lay witnesses are primarily *our* witnesses. They are willing to talk with us and have all sorts of helpful things to say. They also have harmful things to say. Walking into court without learning everything each available witness has to say is like walking into a boxing match with one eye taped shut.

The techniques for working with lay witnesses and clients are beyond the scope of this book, but here are a few pointers I hope will help you change from an office-centered trial lawyer (faxes, motions, and so on) to a witness-centered trial lawyer.

1. **INTERVIEW ALL IMPORTANT WITNESSES BEFORE YOU FILE THE CASE.** Of course, you won't always be able to do this, but it is an important aspiration. The closer you come to this goal, the better you will handle the case. Early interviews will help you frame the issues and causes of action, structure your discovery, and avoid cases you shouldn't take in the first place. In every way, they will put you miles ahead of the defense.

2. **FORM RELATIONSHIPS WITH WITNESSES.** You don't need to become a witness's new best friend, but you should impart a sense that you are reliable and you respect that person. The two of you are going through a unique experience together. Even for experienced witnesses and lawyers, every case is unique. You will be asking witnesses to cooperate with the scheduling problems that always arise in litigation; they need your help understanding an unfamiliar and sometimes frightening process.

    A relationship with witnesses means you treat them like fellow human beings and gain some understanding of how they view the world and their place in it. This will help them become more effective witnesses.

3. **SPEND TIME WITH THE WITNESSES.** Try not to be in a rush. Force yourself to slow down and ignore all the deadlines

crowding in on you. The more time you spend with witnesses, the more you will each learn, and the better you will each do in court.

4. **TELL WITNESSES HOW THEY FIT INTO THE CASE.** You know (or think you know) the whole case and how the pieces fit together. Witnesses see only a small piece of the case. Unless you tell them, they will have no idea how they fit in to the larger whole. We are all uncomfortable if we feel out of context. It is like coming into a classroom for the first time, halfway through the third lesson. If witnesses have an overview of the case and feel you think they are important enough to interview, the chances of their willing participation increase.

5. **ASK OPEN-ENDED QUESTIONS.** Don't make the mistake of being goal-driven when interviewing witnesses. You have a preconceived idea of how a particular witness fits into the case and try to extract the facts from the witness as quickly and efficiently as possible—before moving on to the next legal task. Approaching the interview this way, you will often miss key facts that witnesses know.

Try questions like:
- What stands out most in your mind about the accident? The situation? The drivers?
- Who knows more about this than you do? Was anyone else around?
- How did it feel to witness this?
- What do you think are the most important things for a jury to know about this situation?

Obviously, you will want to follow up and ask for specific details, but you will be amazed at the things you will learn by asking questions that invite witnesses to express what they consider important.

Invite them to tell you the "bad stuff" about your client or "the facts." You might even ask questions like: "What is the worst thing you can tell me about my client?" or, "Do you think my client did the right thing in filing this lawsuit?" Better that you hear it first outside of court than during a deposition or trial.

6. **SPEND MORE THAN ONE SESSION WITH WITNESSES.** After your first interview, go back and spend some more time with each witness. This might be before the witness is deposed, and again before trial. Every time you meet with a witness, you strengthen your relationship. Chances are, you will learn more facts each time as well. That's just the way human nature works.

7. **GO TO DIFFERENT LOCATIONS TO MEET WITNESSES.** Depending on the case and the importance of the witness, consider going to different locations to meet with witnesses. Think about meeting them at their office or home, a coffee shop, the scene of the accident. Each location may bring out different memories or responses from a witness. Yes, you can also meet at your office, but with many witnesses the responses you get will not be as revealing as they would be at other locations.

8. **IF YOU CAN'T ATTEND TO WITNESSES YOURSELF, HAVE SOMEONE ELSE DO IT.** Ideally, you will be the one meeting with all the

witnesses. If you can't or won't do that, have a trusted partner, associate, or staff member do it. Instructions to that
person should include the points above. If the person en-
trusted with this task has good people skills and an ability
to communicate well with you, you can obtain many of
the benefits of meeting with witnesses yourself. This sec-
ond-best approach is still head and shoulders above ignoring the witnesses until the last minute—or ignoring them
altogether.

When all is said and done, witnesses are the beginning and end
of your case. Give them the time and attention they deserve, and you
will be paid back many times over. Treat them as an afterthought,
and you will suffer.

# CHAPTER TWENTY

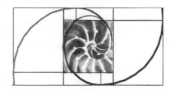

# Jurors Don't Need to Like You or Your Client

Many trial lawyers tell you with conviction that an unlikable client is the kiss of death in a civil case. Given the chance, they will tell you stories of the "perfect case" torpedoed by the client's personality. I am not talking here about lying clients out to cheat the system. I'm talking about genuinely hurt people whom the jury perceives as whiny, angry, mean, coarse, crude, or apathetic. Whatever you do, you cannot pull them far enough out of their misery to have them make a good impression on the jury.

The truth is that trial lawyers win cases for unlikable clients all the time. Is it harder? Yes. Do you have to take greater risks? Yes. Does it always work? No. But unlikable clients need lawyers too. They need a lawyer like you more than most people do.

Try to understand why the clients are the way they are. If their unlikable characteristics stem from their injuries, use this "negative" to enhance your case.[15] If the clients have always been this way, look for the good in them and try to accentuate it. You cannot hide the negatives: "My client is a grouchy old man. Do you think grouchy old men should have rights in the courtroom? Do you think different legal rules should apply to grouchy old men?"

---

15. Friedman, *Polarizing the Case.*

Keep your client's exposure to the jury to a minimum. Whatever facts you need to prove, try to prove through other witnesses and exhibits. In every way you can, attempt to keep the spotlight—the focus of the trial—on your opponent and your opponent's witnesses.

It appears to me that lawyers often attach the "unlikable client" label when they want an excuse to settle, to not take the risks, or to not do the hard work even an unlikable client deserves. Other times, it seems like a post hoc excuse to explain an unexpected loss. And sometimes, I'll be the first to admit, it is absolutely true that despite the trial lawyer's best efforts, the unlikable client loses the case.

What about you? It is very common for unlikable prosecutors and civil defense lawyers to win their cases. They represent authority: the government, large corporations, doctors. In the courtroom, different rules apply to these lawyers than to us. But we too can win cases without being likable.

I am not suggesting you try to be unlikable, but trying to force a personality that just isn't you is a recipe for disaster. Watching lawyers try to ingratiate themselves with a jury is like fingernails on the blackboard for me and, I think, for most jurors. Think about the guy who was rejected on the first date because he was "trying too hard" or the woman we distrust because she is a "people pleaser."

Jurors, like the rest of us, prefer interactions with people who talk with them directly, without artifice, without attempts to create superficial rapport. Their concerns about you have only one dimension—can they trust you as a source of reliable information? If they trust you, they will overlook your unlikable qualities. If they can't trust you as a reliable source of information, all your likability is worthless.

What I have written here should not be your license to act inappropriately in the courtroom. Many of a trial lawyer's unlikable traits are symptoms of a lack of trustworthiness—at least in the jurors' eyes.

To a jury:

- Arrogance = inability to see the case in perspective = unreliable source of information.
- Belligerence = willingness to bully people or facts to get one's way = unreliable source of information.
- Condescension = thinking one is better than others = out of touch with the real world = unreliable source of information.
- Whining = thinking one's facts or case cannot stand up to attack = already thinking one is going to lose = unreliable source of information.

You get the idea. Don't pander. Don't schmooze. Go into the courtroom and do your job presenting your case. Do your job presenting the jurors with information they can rely upon in reaching a verdict for your client. *Trials are not popularity contests—they are reliability contests.*

# CHAPTER TWENTY-ONE

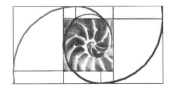

# Embrace Your Conservative Values

Plaintiff's lawyers and criminal defense lawyers often suffer from a misguided sense of moral superiority, ignoring or disdaining some of the more popularly held "conservative" notions. This would simply be annoying and not worth commenting on, if it didn't affect their effectiveness as trial lawyers.

Here I use the loaded term *conservative* as shorthand to connote values, thoughts, and feelings that might energize verdicts against us in court. If three years after a minor injury, our client is not back at work, a conservative thought might be that she is looking for her lawsuit lottery ticket to come in. If our client is a gang member, a conservative thought might be that if he isn't guilty of this crime, he is probably guilty of another and should go to jail. If our client is of Latino heritage, has legally been in the United States for twenty years, and still does not speak English, a conservative thought might be that if she hasn't bothered to learn "our" language, why should we give her "our" rights?

This is a specialized use of the term *conservative,* but will suffice for our purposes. Listen to any conservative talk show or read letters to the editor in your local paper, and you will be exposed to plenty of thoughts and values not only that you oppose, but that might be very harmful to your cases in court. Many trial lawyers dismiss these thoughts and values as rants of the ignorant, prejudiced, and mean-spirited. *This is a huge mistake.*

During a presidential debate, candidate Michael Dukakis was famously asked if his opposition to the death penalty would change if his wife was raped and murdered. His unemotional, intellectual response in opposition to the death penalty turned many voters off and probably contributed to his defeat in the election. Dukakis's failure to imagine or acknowledge his own anger and desire for retribution and revenge—perhaps even to himself—made him unable to connect with his audience or effectively advocate his position. By denying his own very human thoughts and feelings, Dukakis became less credible in advocating a position seemingly at odds with those thoughts and feelings.

How much more credible would Dukakis have appeared if he had said something like:

> *If my wife were raped and murdered, I would want to kill with my bare hands anyone I thought was responsible. I would be in a rage. I would not be thinking clearly. It is quite possible I would make mistakes. That is why I shouldn't be allowed to decide who lives and who dies.*
>
> *As a society, we can also get carried away with rage and horror and make mistakes. As a country, we should try to hold ourselves to higher standards. We should leave vengeance to God and have the humility and humanity to avoid the intentional killing of others—no matter what we think of them.*

Such a response would not likely have persuaded death penalty proponents to change their position. But it might have kept Dukakis from losing the voters who were ambivalent about the death penalty or ambivalent about Dukakis.

Whenever we deny our own conservative thoughts or feelings, we risk looking either dishonest or inhuman. Perhaps even worse, we risk creating our own blind spots, hiding the power of the other side's arguments from ourselves.

If you think about it, most conservative values are not the unique property of conservatives—they are values we all *share*. They are shared, at least, by most people in this country. In every case, some conservative values can work against you, and some can work for you. If you deny that you share these values, you handicap yourself in the courtroom.

In this country, we admire people who work hard. We look down on those looking for a free ride. If, three years after a minor injury, your client is not back at work, the jury will have a predictable, negative reaction. Claiming that you don't share this reaction may make you feel superior, but it is counterproductive. Pretending that the jury should not have this reaction gets you nowhere.

Part of your job is to counsel your client. Explain how the jury will perceive her. Explain that the problem is easily solved by getting back to work. If she can't work at her prior job, she should get *some* type of job—*any job.*

Look for other conservative values that can neutralize or even trump the work ethic. Perhaps the doctors told your client *not* to go back to work until she reached a certain point in her recovery. Maybe the doctors can testify to this as well as to how hard your client has been working to reach that point. Maybe your client has been caring for a sick family member, and that has taken up all her time. As long as you are not claiming lost wages, the jury will readily approve of your client's choice to care for a family member.

Suppose you represent a client of Latino heritage who has been in this country for twenty years and still does not speak English. If you look deep inside yourself, you may find some small part that sympathizes with the view that if she wants the benefits of living in this country, she should learn English. Why hide from that? Why try to pretend you are superior to jurors who hold this view? In *voir dire,* maybe you ask: "Mrs. Garcia has lived here twenty years and never learned English. Does she deserve the right to use our court system?"

Maybe you present evidence of all the English classes she took. Maybe she's one of those people who just has trouble with languages. Maybe you show that she's been working sixty hours per week for the last twenty years and never had time to take an English class. *But she made sure every one of her children learned English.* "You see?" you in effect say to the jury, "The Garcia family is assimilating, just as our American dream would have them do."

If your client is a gang member, look for other facts that put him in a good conservative light. Maybe he has a full-time job, and his employer will testify to how hard he works. Maybe he is a devoted son to his mother. Maybe there is nothing good you can say about him, and you will have to appeal to other conservative values like our right to associate with whomever we like, regardless of what the government thinks about it. My point here is not that you can always find a conservative value to support your case (though you usually can), but that pretending the conservative value is not validly in play or that you don't share that value is the road to disaster.

Look for ways to get in touch with your "inner conservative." When you read a particularly offensive letter to the editor, look deep within yourself and see if there isn't some part of you that responds to the point the writer makes. Watch or listen to conservative television and radio shows. They are speaking to a part of you; pay attention.

Don't worry. You won't turn into Rush Limbaugh. When you acknowledge the force and power of these conservative values, you will see that they can work for you as well as against you. But try to hide from them or hold yourself apart from them, and they will destroy your case.

# CHAPTER TWENTY-TWO

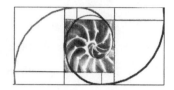

# Silence Can Be Your Friend

In the courtroom, everyone is watching us, listening to us. The judge is peering down over the bench; the jurors are taking notes; our client looks on hopefully; our adversary is watching like a cat, tail twitching, ready to pounce at our first wrong syllable.

It is our job to talk, to fill the silence with persuasive words and argument. So we talk and talk and talk and talk and talk and talk and talk. The jurors drift away, the judge goes back to her e-mail, our adversary relaxes, and our client still looks on hopefully, the only one in the courtroom still hanging on our every word.

Great orators, great trial lawyers, and those with even superficial involvement in theater have always known there is great power in silence. Using silence is in part a technique, and I am determined not to let this become a book about technique. However, most of us have a barrier to using this technique, and I will try to address this barrier here.

The next time you are in court or speaking in public, try to notice how hard it is to purposefully stop talking. I am not referring to the pauses that occur when you transition from one argument to another: "That is why the search was illegal. That leads us to the question of what evidence must be suppressed. [*pause*] The first category consists of documents…" I am also not talking about the pauses that occur, despite your best efforts, when you lose your train of thought.

A purposeful pause is one in which you interrupt the pattern, cadence, or drone of your speech to gather your audience's attention or to emphasize a point. It is one of the most powerful techniques in the courtroom, and one of the least used.

I believe we use it the least because it feels so scary. Paradoxically, it feels as though we are giving up power or control when we stop talking. In fact, we are gathering more power and control, pulling everyone's focus toward us.

This whole concept is difficult to describe on the printed page, but try to see and hear yourself delivering these two versions of the beginning of an opening statement:

## Statement One

*The government's case is based on the testimony of two criminals. The first is John Shaw, a convicted drug dealer, to whom the government paid $20,000 over the last year. The second is Tony Henderson, who has eight felony convictions, including three that specifically involve crimes of dishonesty.*

## Statement Two

*The government's case is based on the testimony of* [pause for a couple of seconds while looking at the jury] *two criminals. The first is John Shaw, a convicted drug dealer, to whom the government paid $20,000 over the last year. The second is Tony Henderson* [pause for a couple of seconds while looking at the jury]. *He has eight felony convictions, including three that specifically involve crimes of dishonesty.*

What happens when you pause? Everything stops. Here's the paradox again: when you *stop* talking, everyone pays attention. You stand before the jury without even words between you. You are bare. If you are sincere, the jury will hear you loud and clear.

Nothing is special about the places where I inserted pauses in the example. Several other places would work equally well or better. In my experience, it is best not to plan your pauses, just consciously try to insert them when it feels right. Yes, I know, at first it will never feel right. Force yourself to do it. Then do it again. *Play* with it.

Try it during oral argument or even when telling a story to a group of friends. But try it. The power of silence is a gift only you can give. Give yourself that gift. Can you overdo silence? Of course. So don't overdo it.

Having trouble getting started? Try a rhetorical question. Rhetorical questions are a good way to begin practicing the power of silence, because they practically cry out for a pause. In oral argument, you might say: "Why do you suppose the defense never disclosed this document before? [*pause*]." In closing argument, you might say to the jury: "Mr. Defense Counsel just argued _____. Is there a single exhibit to support that argument? [*pause*] A single witness? [*pause*]." Once you are comfortable with pausing after rhetorical questions, it will be easier to pause during declarative statements.

As you are getting up the nerve to practice the power of silence, you may want to watch and listen to great trial lawyers who have mastered it.[16] You can order a video of Moe Levine from the AAJ.

---

16. Great political speakers are not useful to watch because their pauses are invariably filled with the sounds of cheers and clapping. This is an expected part of their forum, and one that deprives the silence of the power and magic at the disposal of the trial lawyer.

It is worth watching for many reasons.[17] Watch it several times. At least one of those times, pay close attention to his masterful use of silence. You don't need to be Moe Levine to tap into this power. You just need the courage to stop talking.

---

17. *Comparative Closing Arguments on Damages,* featuring Marvin E. Lewis and Moe Levine (ATLA Video, 1993).

# CHAPTER TWENTY-THREE

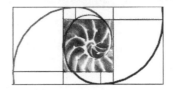

# You Must Ask for Money

Some lawyers have a particularly difficult time asking the jury for money. Arguments for recovery of lost wages and medical expenses are easy because concrete evidence of a particular amount has been introduced. That number is easy to discuss. But what about figures for mental and emotional distress, loss of consortium, pain and suffering? Here any amounts we talk about are necessarily arbitrary and subjective. This characteristic makes many lawyers nervous about arguing these elements of damages. They feel as though they are on thin ice.

They are. There is no question that jurors are more resistant to awarding money for these types of injuries than for lost wages or medical expenses. There is also no question that you cannot prove the value of these types of injuries the same way you can prove lost wages or medical expenses.

Some lawyers respond to this problem by not asking the jury for a specific dollar amount for these injuries. This is usually a mistake. Let's start with the most common situation in which you *should avoid* asking for a specific dollar amount.

Suppose you have tried a wrongful termination of employment case, and you have proven $1 million in past and future wage loss.

You and your client would be thrilled to win a liability verdict and $1 million in wage loss. You also have a claim for emotional and mental distress. Your client was upset at losing his job. He was embarrassed and humiliated. He worried about paying his bills. However, he got another job and landed on his feet. Although he is angry at being fired, there is no apparent lasting harm. If liability is a close call, you might be better off barely mentioning the emotional and mental distress claim. Keep the focus on the facts and claims most important to you—and those most likely to move the jury.

In any case in which you have a big, provable special damages claim, say for lost wages, and a relatively minor claim for emotional distress, you may not want to talk much about the emotional distress claim. Doing so risks taking the jurors' attention away from your strong main claim. This main claim will be diluted by a subjective claim which the jury is resistant to. If liability is close, you don't want to spend your credibility arguing for what the jurors perceive to be a weak, minor claim.

You may even want to enhance your credibility with the jury by saying something like:

> *The judge has instructed you that Sam is entitled to recover for the emotional and mental distress they put him through when they fired him. He had to tell his parents he'd lost his job; he had to worry each month if he could pay the bills. But he handled it. That's the kind of person he is. And he is fine now. If your verdict reflects the wages they took from him, he doesn't need anything else. I would suggest that on this line in the verdict form you enter _____, to reflect that what they did was wrong. They caused him harm.*

Maybe you will suggest $10, maybe $10,000. The point you'll be making is the same—emotional damage is not what the case is about.

In cases in which success depends on obtaining significant awards for general damages such as mental and emotional distress, you are much more likely to be happy with the result if you ask for a specific amount of money. Many lawyers have obtained large general damages awards *without* asking for specific amounts; I have myself. Still, your chances of success are greater if you give the jury a specific number.

Jurors are already skeptical of these types of damages claims. Your unwillingness to look them in the eye and ask for a specific amount sends the message that you too are uneasy about these claims. If you tell them the equivalent of, "Do what you think is fair," they will interpret this halfhearted effort as an admission the claims lack merit.

Jurors assume the lawyers know the true value of each claim. Your allies on the jury are looking to you for guidance. Your adversaries on the jury are looking for signs of weakness. Failing to give a number is a sign of weakness.

Help the jurors who want to help your client. By the time of closing argument, you should be their trusted leader and guide. Show them you are not afraid of putting a fair number on the claim, so they're not afraid to do the same.

One of the biggest impediments to asking for a specific dollar amount for general damages is the difficulty of finding the "right number." Let me say again. *Jurors assume you know the true value of the claim.* In their minds, you are an expert. You have handled similar claims, you have read about similar claims, you have settled similar claims. They are watching and listening to you closely, trying to decipher the fair value of the claim—based upon your words and conduct.

Jurors also assume that, as an advocate, you may ask for more than the fair value—or at least the high end of reasonable. They will not hold that against you, so long as you do not ask for a ridiculous amount. Ask for $1 million for the pain and suffering of a broken arm, and you are likely to be in trouble.

What is ridiculous and what is reasonable? This will vary from case to case and from jurisdiction to jurisdiction. I suggest asking yourself the same question you are asking the jurors to answer. Knowing what you know and with the responsibility to be fair to *both* sides, what would you award? Then I would suggest scaling that amount back slightly. Not because it is too much, but to ensure that when you look the jurors in the eye, you are confident what you are asking for is fair and right.

I know, it is hard. In case you haven't noticed by now, most of this book is about getting you to do the hard thing, when human nature pushes you toward the easy thing. Here are some suggestions to help you along.

## Look for Benchmarks

Often, objectively provable items of damage are in the case. You can compare the value of these items to general damages. In an employment case, you might say:

> *Joe wanted to be a police officer since he was fifteen years old. You heard how hard he worked. First in his class at the academy. Commendation after commendation. This was not just a job; this was who he was. It was all he ever wanted to be, and they took that from him. He will never be a police officer again.*

> *You have heard how he has struggled to rebuild his life. That is a real loss, which the law requires you to consider and compensate for. It is not as easy to calculate as lost wages, but I suggest to you that when they fired Joe, they took more than his paycheck; they took his identity, his pride, his place in our society. That loss is at least equal to the paycheck they took.*

If you had $500,000 in lost wages, you just asked for another $500,000 in mental and emotional distress. Wasn't that easy?

In a personal injury case, you might say something like:

> *There was more to Bill's life than the paycheck he earned. The paycheck allowed him to financially survive. What gave his life meaning? Fishing with his daughters every weekend. Dancing with his wife on Saturday night. Hunting with his friends in the fall. This was his joy, his reward for hard work. This is what he valued above all.*
>
> *All these things have been taken from him. If you give him back his paycheck, you allow him to financially survive, but you have not compensated him for his most serious loss. I suggest that these losses are at least equal to the loss of his paycheck.*

Without lost wages, look for other benchmarks, maybe the medical expenses now necessary to keep the plaintiff healthy. Maybe some random fact that has come out at trial:

> *You heard that the tractor trailer that crashed into Dave's car was worth $200,000. I suggest that the pain and suffering he will experience for the rest of his life is at least equal to the value of that truck. Does anyone doubt that if Dave had that $200,000, he would gladly trade it for a life free from pain?*

I am not suggesting that pointing to a benchmark is all you need do to get a large general damages award. You should read the great arguments of other trial lawyers, read their books, and come up with your own arguments about the importance of these intangible, but very real losses. The single best source on the subject is David Ball's revolutionary book *David Ball on Damages*.[18]

The benchmark is simply a tool, used by trial lawyers for over a century, to overcome a lawyer's natural reluctance to name a specific number. It is also an effective way to get the jurors thinking of the right order of magnitude when evaluating general damages.[19]

If you have trouble saying "$900,000" and "pain and suffering" in the same sentence, another technique is to *write* the numbers instead of speak them. Enlarge the verdict form to poster size, or write your own version on the blackboard or whiteboard. Maybe it would look like this:

$_____ Past lost wages

$_____ Future lost wages

$_____ Past pain and suffering

$_____ Future pain and suffering

$_____ Past mental and emotional distress

$_____ Future mental and emotional distress

Explain to the jurors that they will be required to fill out this verdict form and consider each of these elements of damages. Then explain how past lost wages were proven and are calculated. Write that amount in the blank. Do the same for future lost wages.

---

18. David Ball, *David Ball on Damages: The Essential Update,* 2d ed. (NITA, 2006). Many of the points in this chapter are explained more clearly and in more detail in Ball's book. Also take a look at Jim M. Perdue, *Who Will Speak for the Victim?* (State Bar of Texas, 1989), an encyclopedia of good plaintiff's arguments.

19. There are now social science studies confirming that the benchmark approach has a very real impact on juror thinking. Faced with the ambiguous, standardless task of calculating general damages, the human mind looks for something, anything, to latch on to as a standard of comparison. *Help the jurors. Give them something.*

When you get to pain and suffering, explain what that is. Explain the evidence that applies. Do the same with mental and emotional distress. Then you might say something like:

> We live in a time when people are being paid five or ten million a year to play games like baseball or basketball. On television, people win a million dollars for answering eight questions or picking the right briefcase.
>
> As Bill's lawyer, I can write any number in these blanks. But he is not an athlete or a celebrity. He's just a construction worker who will live in pain the rest of his life. He will never take his daughters fishing again. He doesn't want charity or a windfall. He just wants you to place a fair value on the things that have been taken from him. This is what I suggest is fair.

Then write the amounts in the blanks. Isn't that easy?

If you won't take the risk of *suggesting* an amount, why should the jurors take the greater risk of *awarding* an amount?

# CHAPTER TWENTY-FOUR

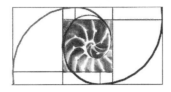

# Superstition

*In this legal world of words, over 90 percent of the impact is
in our nonverbal communication.*

—ALASKA BAR ASSOCIATION BROCHURE DESCRIBING A SEMINAR,
*Powerful Communication Inside the Courtroom and Out*

I won my first civil trial wearing a red and blue striped necktie. As the years went by, it was clear to me that I did better in court when I wore that tie. But was I winning at trial *because* of that tie or *despite* it? Or was the tie making any difference at all?

How can we possibly know what does and does not work in the courtroom? When I "Polarize" a case[20] and win, did I win because of the Polarizing approach, or would I have had a better verdict without it? There is no way to scientifically test this. There is no objective standard against which we can measure trial techniques or performance.

One result of this enigma is that lawyers will latch onto anything that appears to explain the results in a case. If I know why I won or lost the last case, I should be able to control the outcome in the next case by doing the same thing again, right?

---

20. Friedman, *Polarizing the Case.*

Lawyers work on a case, learning the facts and the law. But this is not a neutral, dispassionate, scholarly search for knowledge and understanding. Lawyers are looking for weapons. They are looking for facts, law, and arguments that will help win the case. Of course, being human, lawyers fall in love with the facts, law, and arguments they found or "created." If they win the case, they are convinced they won *because* of what they did.

I know a well-known, highly successful trial lawyer who almost always tells a particular story in closing argument. To me, it is a pointless story that can't possibly help him win. He obviously believes the jury responds to the story. We will never know who is right.

If the jury rejects a lawyer's techniques and arguments, the lawyer can only conclude something irrational has occurred. If the jury is irrational, where can the trial lawyer turn? To the modern religion of social science and the growth industry of trial consultants.[21]

There trial lawyers learn that a blue suit signals authority and power; a brown suit, credibility. They learn that they can program jurors like Pavlov's dogs. If they stand in the same place every time they make a particular point, pretty soon they can stop saying anything and simply stand at their "anchor point" to communicate to the jury. And yes, they learn that 90 percent of communication is nonverbal.

The unspoken message is if we simply dress right, use the right gestures, stand in the right place, and have the right tone and graphics, we will win, no matter what nonsense comes out of our mouths. (I wonder what the speaker at the above-cited lecture would communicate if he spent 90 percent of his time at the lectern with his mouth closed and his body gyrating?)

---

21. Some of my best friends are trial consultants. Dynamic, creative, insightful people, they can have much to offer the trial lawyer. However, some trial consultants are mediocre, incompetent, or outright charlatans.

Postverdict interviews with jurors can be particularly misleading. They remind me of the written evaluations from people who attend my seminars. One evaluator may say a particular part of my presentation was quite good, and three others may say they hated it. One juror may tell you that your Power Point presentation was powerful; another may say it was a complete waste of time.

A few quick points to consider about postverdict interviews:

1. You rarely talk to all of the jurors.

2. You usually talk to those jurors most friendly to your cause.

3. Jurors are polite and don't like to offend anyone.

4. Jurors themselves often don't know or can't say why they made decisions. They may well rationalize to themselves before they rationalize to you.

Whenever you present to a group of people who then go off and make a decision together, their self-reported reasoning is suspect. Yet I have heard countless lawyers report what a juror said to them as if they had discovered the Holy Grail of trial advocacy. (Yes, I've done it myself.)

This problem of not knowing what causes trial results can drive you to distraction. The trial lawyer clings with religious fervor to Irving Younger's *Ten Commandments of Cross-examination,* a favorite trial consultant's opinions about "trial as theater," or a random comment from a juror five trials ago. There may be wisdom in these teachings. But blind adherence to trial dogma, whether you or others create it, won't bring the results you want—no matter how reassuring the dogma is.

Here is my most unscientific advice. Listen to jury consultants, perform focus groups, interview jurors post-trial, and read Younger's

*Ten Commandments.* All are helpful—*to inform your own intuition and judgment.* In the end, your own intuition and judgment are your most important resources. Treat them with care and respect.

Pay attention to what *feels* as if it is working in the courtroom. What *feels* as though it is not working? Usually, you can tell what is working and what isn't, if your mind is not preoccupied with following a rigid script for trial performance.

Use your rational judgment to *analyze* what is working in the courtroom.

- Was the cross-examination as good as it felt?
- Was the witness as important as I thought?
- What other factors in the case were more important to the jury than discrediting this witness?

With experience, your intuition and judgment will improve. Good trial lawyers have learned how to harness *both* in the service of their clients. You will never find the Holy Grail. Your best hope is for continued improvement and the strength to keep trying.

Yes, it is frustrating and difficult. If you need a pat formula to be comfortable in your job, trial lawyering might not be for you.

Part III

# *At Home in the Jungle*

A TIME WILL COME WHEN YOU BEGIN TO THINK OF YOURSELF AS A TRIAL lawyer. It may be after your first trial or your twentieth. It will dawn on you that you are living the life of a trial lawyer; you *are* a trial lawyer.

About this time, you'll realize that being a trial lawyer presents plenty of challenges outside of the courtroom as well as within it. The line between outside and inside the courtroom gets blurry. You are a trial lawyer when you address the jury; you are also a trial lawyer when you teach your child how to ride a bike. You are a mother when you argue to the judge; you are a mother when you attend a parent-teacher conference.

You are a whole person, and you have chosen an occupation that *demands* you be a whole person to be effective. At the same time, it's a job that can cause you to lose touch with yourself and isolate you from those who mean the most to you. This part of the book addresses some of the challenges you will face as you settle into your life as a trial lawyer.

# CHAPTER TWENTY-FIVE

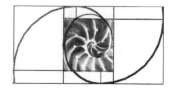

# Therapy

*The task of psychotherapy is to help the person achieve, through a special relationship with a therapist, good communication within himself. Once this is achieved, he can communicate more freely and more effectively with others.*

—CARL R. ROGERS, *On Becoming a Person*

A friend of mine says no one can be a great trial lawyer without going to therapy. I disagree, but would say that, whatever your potential as a trial lawyer, you are more apt to fully realize it by going to therapy. You're more likely to be happy too.

If, as Oliver Wendell Holmes said, "The law is a jealous mistress," then trial law is an angry pit bull, shackled to your ankle.

Of course, you are shackled to yourself—to your own psychological wounds that caused you to become a trial lawyer in the first place. Those wounds give you energy and motivation. They can also be your undoing.

Maybe you have no psychological wounds—at least that you're aware of. Still, you are shackled to your own sense of self—call it your personality—and a job that will rip and tear at the slightest weakness in your emotional makeup. And we all have weaknesses in our emotional makeup.

I am no psychologist. In trying to explain why therapy might help you, I am being overly simplistic. A psychologist could easily refute parts of what I say. That doesn't matter. I am communicating with you as one person to another, offering you a framework for thinking about the benefits of therapy. Although the discussion may be psychologically incomplete or somewhat inaccurate, it's a good model for thinking about these issues.

Let's start with your personality, or sense of self. What is it made of? For present purposes, think of your "self" as made up of:

1. Traits or characteristics
2. Parts of your history or story
3. Thoughts and opinions
4. Feelings and emotions

## Your Traits or Characteristics

A large part of your self is made up of a potentially infinite number of traits or characteristics. For example, you might be someone who either seeks or avoids:

1. Working under pressure, against a deadline
2. Confrontation
3. Competition
4. Large groups of people
5. Authority
6. Humor
7. Intellectual challenge
8. Public exposure of self
9. Risk

Are you shy, optimistic, serious, or anxious? Concerned with appearances or preoccupied with financial security?

Although the list of traits or characteristics is potentially infinite, most of us have a fairly short list we would use to describe ourselves. Where did this list come from? The short answer is that we constructed these traits and characteristics early in life as our own sense of self emerged. Let's avoid the whole nature versus nurture discussion here. Whatever your genetic makeup, you found yourself in a particular environment. As you exhibited certain traits or characteristics, you received feedback from your environment.

Perhaps you discovered that confronting the people in your life got you what you wanted. Confrontation became a positive value for you. On the other hand, maybe confrontation only brought turmoil and unhappiness, so you learned to avoid it. Humor may have brought you joy or comfort or eased tension. Humor may have been aggression or anger in disguise. As a result, you chose what part humor would play in your sense of self.

If you think about the traits or characteristics you would choose to describe yourself, it will probably be easy to see how these characteristics served you well in childhood and adolescence. More important to our present discussion, think about the traits and characteristics you would use to describe yourself at age sixteen and those you would use to describe yourself now. How different are they? If you are like most people, there is not much difference.

Where does that leave you? First, you *chose* the traits and characteristics that make up your personality, or sense of self. Second, you chose these traits and characteristics in the first ten to fifteen years of your life. That's right, you are walking around in the adult world—and walking around in the courtroom—with a personality constructed by a child.

## Parts of Your History or Story

In a legal case, the lawyers select from an almost infinite number of facts the ones they consider material, or important to telling the story. The material facts give the story meaning. In an auto rollover case, for example, the plaintiff's lawyer will not have the factory worker who attached the rearview mirror testify. What the worker did was relevant in the sense that he worked on the car, but what he did was immaterial to the story of why the car rolled over.

The same thing happens as you construct the narrative of your life that you carry around with you. Out of all the things that have happened to you, you select relatively few to become part of your story and, therefore, your sense of self. One person may be poor at athletics, and that becomes a critical part of his or her story. Another may be poor at athletics, and this receives no mention at all.

Most of us carry more than one version of our story around with us. We might tell one version to someone we meet casually at a party, another version at a job interview, and still another to our spouse. Just as we choose what version of our story to tell others, we also choose what version to tell ourselves, about ourselves.

Some events are so profound that they seem to *demand* a presence in our story, a mother dying when we are thirteen, for example. Even then, we choose what meaning to give that event.

If we pay attention, the *meaning* we give to events in our history may evolve and change over time. Usually, without therapy or a major disruption in our life's course, the story we tell ourselves about ourselves does not change very much over time. New events are added, of course, as our lives unfold, but once events and their meaning are in our story, they tend not to change very much.

That's right, another major element of your personality—the

meaning you give to events—was constructed before you were old enough to legally drink beer.

## Your Thoughts and Opinions

Many of us rely heavily on our thoughts and opinions to give us a sense of self. Our traits, characteristics, and the story we tell about ourselves heavily influence the thoughts and opinions to which we gravitate. This is easier to observe in others than in ourselves. Listen to focus group members or jurors describing their opinions, and you will soon hear them recounting their own stories or personal characteristics to justify their opinions.

I am not concerned here with how we form our thoughts and opinions, but rather with how strongly we identify with our thoughts and opinions. People are willing to kill or be killed over thoughts and opinions. Family members will refuse to speak to each other because of differing opinions about religion. I am a Democrat. When I hear you are a Republican, I am on guard and defensive—my sense of self is threatened.

I cling to my thoughts and opinions because I perceive them to be part of me. If a contrary thought or opinion threatens me, how can I accurately perceive it?

## Your Feelings and Emotions

From earliest childhood, we are taught to keep our feelings and emotions in check. Certain feelings or emotions make others uncomfortable; we try to hide them. Other feelings or emotions may make *us* uncomfortable; we try to deny or suppress them.

A variety of factors, from the personal to the cultural, can cause us to lose touch with our feelings. But feelings don't go away. They just go underground and manipulate us surreptitiously.

Suppose I was raised by a single mother. We were very close. In addition to a variety of positive traits, my mother was controlling and tyrannical. I am able to acknowledge what I consider the positive aspects of my mother's parenting, but I have denied the anger and resentment I felt and still feel because of my mother's actions. I might tell you I had a great mother and that I have nothing but positive feelings for her. Yet when I am in front of a female judge who corrects me in some way, I feel anger and resentment far out of proportion to the situation. I may even speak or act far out of proportion to the situation.

My feelings are controlling me, whether I acknowledge them or not. More accurately, my feelings are controlling me *because* I will not acknowledge them.

Yes, sorry to say, many of these unacknowledged feelings, which secretly control our behavior, had their genesis in childhood. Even those that developed later are usually suppressed and unacknowledged because of traits and characteristics developed during childhood.

"So what?" you might fairly ask. "Everyone is walking around with personalities they formed in childhood, telling themselves stories about themselves, holding tightly to their opinions and hiding from their feelings. That's what humans do." You're right. At least that's what most humans do. But most humans aren't trying to become trial lawyers.

Two things make you different. First, you've chosen a career that requires you to clearly see and feel what is going on with other people. Second, you've chosen a career that will subject you to enormous conflict and pressure. Let's address each of these in turn.

## Seeing Clearly

According to psychologist Carl Rogers:

> *Psychological research has shown that if the evidence*
> *of our sense runs contrary to our picture of self, then*
> *that evidence is distorted. In other words, we cannot*
> *see what our senses report, but only the things which*
> *fit the picture we have.*[22]

How can I hope to hear what the prospective juror is telling me, if I am preoccupied with how I look? A voice in my head keeps saying, "Your ears are too big, and everyone in the audience can see." How can I respond to the judge's concerns about my argument when I am filled with anger—anger whose source I can't pinpoint? If my way of dealing with stress is to crack jokes, if that is what comforts and makes me feel at ease, how will I see that my jokes are falling flat in the courtroom? Just as Carl Rogers said and countless psychological studies have confirmed, our sense of self distorts our perception of what is going on around us.

In many ways, the distortion can be comforting. Maybe I am more comfortable worrying about whether my ears are too big—an old familiar worry I am used to dealing with—than worrying about how this prospective juror will view my case. I might prefer to be angry at the judge—even if I can't clearly articulate why—than to do the hard work of figuring out the merits in the judge's viewpoint.

We formed our selves to deal with a reality that no longer exists—or at least *largely* no longer exists. It's as if we spent our first twenty years in a small room doing close-up work on watches and jewelry, wearing thick lenses to help us see clearly. Now we are

---

22. Carl Rogers, *On Becoming a Person* (Houghton Mifflin, 1995), 115.

outside, driving a car at sixty miles per hour, still wearing those thick lenses designed for close-up work.

Simply stated, our sense of self creates blind spots and distorts of perception. We don't see ourselves as we really are (perhaps we're afraid to), and we are unable to see others as they really are. As events unfold, we are often reacting to unexplored things inside of us rather than to the events themselves.

Therapy can help you become more aware of your own blind spots and distortions. For most of us, those blind spots never entirely go away. But as you begin to see yourself and others more clearly, you will become a more effective trial lawyer. I guarantee it.

## Conflict and Pressure

Other than a combat soldier's or a police officer's, it is hard to think of a job with more intensity, conflict, and pressure than that of a trial lawyer. These conflicts and pressures are vastly different from what most of us experienced when we were creating our personalities. It is common for beginning trial lawyers to feel overwhelmed, scared, panicked, incompetent, nauseous, angry, resentful, exhausted, anxious, and depressed, to name just a few.

You can hide from these feelings with alcohol or drugs. You can detach from these feelings and, in the process, detach from yourself and those you love. However you handle these feelings, as time goes on, if you do not address them directly, they take on a life of their own. More accurately, they take on *your* life, controlling it in ways that are neither pleasant nor helpful.

You can deal with these feelings in ways other than therapy; therapy with a good therapist is just more reliable. A good therapist will help you bring these feelings out into the open, where they lose much of their power to control you.

## Results of Therapy

There is no guarantee therapy will do you any good. But some of the changes that have been shown to occur in therapy include increased self-confidence and self-acceptance and becoming more mature and less rigid in perception. "[The person] becomes more open to the evidence, both to what is going on outside of himself, and to what is going on inside of himself."[23]

Who wouldn't want any or all of these things? You won't get any of them overnight or even in a few months. But eventually, you should see changes. These changes cannot help but make you a better trial lawyer.

## Finding a Therapist

A bad therapist is worse than a waste of time. I am no expert on selecting a therapist, but here are a few things I believe are true.

The therapeutic relationship is a very personal one. You are looking for someone you can trust, someone with whom you feel at ease. Don't be afraid to change therapists until you find someone with whom you "click." A good therapist is someone who can push you to reveal things about yourself that you were only dimly aware of before.

Ask friends and relatives about their experiences. If someone you respect says a therapist has helped him or her, that's an encouraging sign. Ask prospective therapists about their philosophies and methods. What do they hope to do for you? How will they go about it?

Therapy is expensive. If you cannot afford a therapist, consider group therapy. It is cheaper and often as effective, and it will expose

---

23. Rogers, *On Becoming a Person*, 280–81.

you to the interior lives of others. This latter benefit, all by itself, will make you a better trial lawyer.

You don't have to appear at the therapist office with a problem. If you have one, great. Otherwise, tell your prospective therapist that you want to become a better trial lawyer, and you think therapy will help. It will.

# CHAPTER TWENTY-SIX

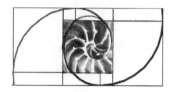

# Winning

*I don't laugh when I win, so that I don't have to cry when I lose.*

—GAIL FRATIES, ALASKA TRIAL LAWYER

Winning feels good. Losing feels bad. Some lawyers, me included, report they don't feel joy at winning, simply relief that they did not lose.

What does it mean to "win" a case? It means you worked hard and made some good decisions. But when you lose, you probably also worked hard and made some good decisions.

It's hard to keep a sense of perspective about winning. On one hand, you should be proud of your hard work and good decisions. On the other hand, plenty of other lawyers probably could have won the case as well. Plenty would have lost it too. What does it mean that you won?

Undoubtedly, circumstances beyond your control played a part in your victory: the jury's makeup, defense counsel's conduct, the defense's decision to try the case instead of settle, the judge's rulings, and others. It may be easy to get a $10 million verdict for a particular case in downtown Los Angeles and impossible to even win the same case in South Dakota.

Honestly appraising trial results leads to the conclusion that comparing trial lawyers' performance is an exercise in self-delusion. A trial has too many moving parts to make comparisons valid. I suggest that to assess the meaning of a victory, you are better off not comparing your victory to other lawyers' victories or defeats. Someone may have obtained a verdict of more or less in a similar case, but that really tells you nothing.

Look instead to the client and the history of your case. Was it a difficult case? (They almost all are.) Did you beat the civil defense's or prosecution's offer? If you can answer yes to both questions, you can take pride in having helped your client obtain a good result. If you wish you had done better, you can learn your lessons from this trial and strive to do better next time. If you had a spectacular result, you can be thankful for all the intangible and unknowable factors that helped you get that result.

My purpose in this short chapter is to warn you about a pitfall that can result from winning one trial or several trials in a row. Winning a difficult case can make you feel competent and powerful. You have overcome adversity, demonstrated your trial powers, and proven that you know better than the naysayers. The danger, of course, is hubris. It can sneak up on you, despite your best efforts, if you are on a winning streak. You will be tempted to take cases you should reject, reject settlement offers you should take, and ignore advice you should heed. Then you will fall—hard.

Enjoy winning. You worked hard for it. But recognize you only played a *part* in the outcome. And you will only play a part in the outcome of your next trial. And the ones after that.

# CHAPTER TWENTY-SEVEN

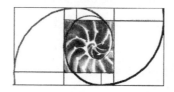

# Losing

*Achievement at the highest level is about recovering from failure.*

—GIO VALIENTE, PH.D.

Much has been written about the causes for the decline in the number of jury trials. One cause I have not seen discussed is a psychological one. We live in a culture in which, as humorist Garrison Keillor says, "all the children are above average." In our culture, there is a bright line between winners and losers, and losers are expected to get an extreme makeover. In this culture, we regard the risk of losing with almost pathological terror.

I hate losing as much as the next person. Nothing is quite like putting your heart, soul, and mind into a trial and then having a jury reject it all. I go to great lengths to avoid losing. There is a difference, however, between going to great lengths to avoid losing and going to great lengths to avoid the *risk* of losing.

In our risk-averse society, most people—including lawyers—want a no-risk, predictable case, career, marriage, child, life, society, you name it. In this culture, the risk of going to trial and possibly *losing* is for many people terrifying and simply unacceptable.

It was not always so. In the not so distant past, even general practitioners could count on having one or two trials a year. "Litigators" could count on more than that. With that many trials going on, a lawyer could *count on* losing a trial from time to time.

This was not regarded as a bad thing—either personally or professionally. Life—and the law—could be expected to deliver some hard knocks. But much could be learned and even accomplished through losing. Remember *To Kill a Mockingbird?* Remember the Alamo? Some of Clarence Darrow's most eloquent and lasting closing arguments were in cases he lost.

We often learn more from our losses than our victories. They force us to examine our assumptions, decisions, and conduct more closely. That is a good thing. Put yourself under a microscope. Reexamine all of your assumptions about the case. Reevaluate your decisions. Then remember, just as you are never the sole cause of victory, you are almost never the sole cause of defeat.

Your client had someone who believed in her and fought hard for her. Some people never get that from anyone in their life. Some of my most grateful clients have been those whose trials were lost, despite our intense efforts.

You are stronger and smarter for having done the trial you lost. Your future clients will benefit. If you can't handle losing at trial, become a medical malpractice defense lawyer or a prosecutor.

# CHAPTER TWENTY-EIGHT

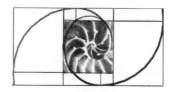

# Settlement

The issue of when or whether to settle bedevils trial lawyers as much as any other issue. It's an easy decision when the client has strong feelings about what should be done with respect to settlement. A competent, well-informed client is entitled to make the decision to accept or reject a settlement offer.

It's more difficult when the client looks to us for advice. In most cases, the client will turn to us, the trusted lawyer, and say, "What do you think I should do?" We sense or know the client will do what we recommend. The client is entitled to know what we believe to be the best course of action. That's one of the reasons we were hired.

Some lawyers try to shirk this responsibility by listing the pros and cons of settling, but are careful not to make a recommendation. If things go badly, they can then say, "It was the client's decision." As a legal matter, it always *is* the client's decision—and the client needs to know that. As a practical matter, in most cases, lawyers weight the outcome of the decision-making process by what they do and don't say. Don't hide from that reality.

How do we know what to recommend? First, we need to recognize some realities about the settlement process.

■ **CLIENTS AND LAWYERS OFTEN HAVE A CONFLICT OF INTEREST.** This is not necessarily an ethical or legal conflict of interest, but a practical one. Lawyers may have an interest in settling immediately so they can pay their mortgage, even if that is not in the client's best interest. Conversely, from a selfish point of view, it may be best for lawyers to go to trial. They can afford the risk of losing, and if they win, fame and wealth could follow.

■ **THE LEGAL SYSTEM ALMOST NEVER FULLY COMPENSATES A PLAINTIFF.** There is a "lawsuit lottery" in this country, but not the one the media discusses. The sad truth is that, of all the people hurt through others' carelessness, virtually none receive full compensation for their injuries. Even if a plaintiff is lucky enough to win a verdict awarding full and fair damages, at least a third of the money goes to the attorney for fees and costs. A plaintiff's chances of being fully compensated are not very different from the chances of winning a lottery. This means that you must view a "successful" outcome in relative, not absolute, terms.

■ **MANY PLAINTIFFS ARE FINANCIALLY DESPERATE.** This means an amount of money may be available in settlement that will make a major positive difference in plaintiff's life—but is still grossly inadequate in terms of fair compensation for the client's injuries. Defense attorneys know this well and use it repeatedly to their advantage. Offers based on this logic are maddening to most plaintiff's attorneys.

Let's consider a hypothetical situation to illustrate these points. You represent a twenty-year-old paraplegic. The liability case is strong. You estimate you have an 80 percent chance of winning on liability. Your economist estimates lost wages at $2 million. Your life-care plan for future care and medical expenses is $5 million. You even have a punitive damages claim, which you estimate has a 50 percent chance of success.

Your client lives with her parents, who are caring for her. She would like to move out and start her own life. The defense offers $3 million in settlement, and you are convinced they will offer no more. You tell all this to the client and her parents. They ask what you think they should do.

Plenty of lawyers, afraid of trial, would quickly settle this case, explaining to the client that this was in her best interests. Others would reject this offer out of hand (with the client's permission, of course) and charge ahead to trial. They would explain to the client that the offer is less than half of her full damages and that justifies rejecting the offer.

What should you do? Don't ask me. I can tell you that I have heard famous lawyers with decades of experience and innumerable multimillion-dollar verdicts agonize over this type of situation. If you settle, you feel like a wimp. If you go to trial, you risk, in retrospect, looking reckless and grandiose to yourself and your client.

Here is the only advice I feel comfortable giving:

- **BE AS HONEST AS YOU CAN IN EXAMINING YOUR OWN MOTIVATIONS.** Only by bringing your motivations out in the open do you have a chance of protecting your client against them. Do you need the money? Do you have a vacation planned at the same time trial is scheduled? Do you want to teach the defense lawyer or the judge a lesson? How big a part should your motivations play in the settlement decision?

- **BE AS HONEST AS YOU CAN IN DETERMINING WHAT IS IN YOUR CLIENT'S BEST INTERESTS.** Your client will live with this decision the rest of her life. What would you tell her if she were your sister or daughter? This is the best question I know to put a trial lawyer in the right frame of mind for evaluating a settlement offer. Another mental game I play with myself, and sometimes the client, is to write on a piece of paper, "$2 million." Then I say, "This is the check you will get in thirty days if you accept the offer. If you turn down this offer, we may double or triple this amount, or you may get nothing." Then I explain my evaluation of the chances of getting nothing and of beating the offer.

In the end, clients will still often look at you and say, "What do you think I should do?" Knowing everything you know about them and their case, you need to tell them.

I've been talking about settling civil cases, but criminal cases have analogous problems. Do you take the deal or don't you? What financial or other personal motivations could be clouding your judgment—or your client's? Are you overreacting to unfairness because the government can pressure your client toward a plea that the evidence does not warrant? Again, if this was your brother or sister, what would you say?

# CHAPTER TWENTY-NINE

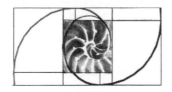

# Physical Health

Make no mistake, trials are physically demanding. Among other things, they are often battles of will and stamina. Who has the stamina at 2:00 A.M. to write one more brief? Who has the will to look back through the documents one more time, trying to develop another line of cross-examination?

As you age, you will rely more on skill and experience. Tasks that once took eight hours may now take one. Unfortunately, as the years go by and experience and skill increase, your stamina will slowly leak away, like air out of an old balloon. Yet you will still find yourself up at 2:00 A.M., dealing with some issue that arose for the first time the day before.

I have seen lawyers so exhausted they could barely string two sentences together in court; so wobbly with fatigue, they looked like punch-drunk fighters, barely able to stand. I have been in that condition myself more than I like to remember.

If you don't take care of your health, you will not be the trial lawyer you could be. Moreover, trial practice will *ruin* your health if you don't make conscious efforts to take care of yourself.

You don't need to be an athlete or a superb physical specimen. I am just talking about the basics here—the things you read about every day: eat sensibly, exercise regularly, and get enough sleep. If you do these things when you are *not* in trial, your mind and body will be more forgiving when you ignore them—if you have to—*during* trial. If all the usual arguments have not convinced you to lead a healthy lifestyle, do it to become a better trial lawyer.

# CHAPTER THIRTY

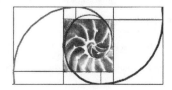

# Family and Friends

Becoming a trial lawyer will affect every relationship you have. How do you maintain close, healthy relationships with people you care about, while at the same time spending most of your waking hours locked in nasty struggles with talented opponents? I wish I had the wisdom to give you a simple, straightforward answer. I don't. But I can warn you of two traps I have seen many lawyers fall into, with the hope you can avoid them.

These traps lie at either end of a continuum. At one end is the trap of emotional entitlement. At the other is the trap of excessive guilt.

## The Trap of Emotional Entitlement

You have a very difficult job. People's lives and well-being depend on your performing at your best. You work extraordinarily hard against long odds to fight for the good people you represent, for causes and issues you believe in, against well-funded, well-organized, merciless opponents.

Your opponents are after you all the time. Take a vacation, and they will file a new motion the day you leave; make the slightest misstatement in a letter or deposition, and you will see it thrown back at you in an opponent's brief; let your guard down for a minute, and one of your opponents will strike from an unexpected angle. You are embattled, heroic, and righteous.

Surely, your superhuman efforts and sacrifices entitle you to a little slack from your family and friends. Of course you are irritable when you get home. Any spouse with an ounce of empathy would understand why. Of course you don't have time to talk to your friend as she goes through a divorce; you are busy helping other people much worse off than her. Of course you don't have the energy to read your daughter a story at bedtime; she'll understand when she grows up and learns of the important work you are doing.

You are a good person—an extraordinary person, doing extraordinary things. The ordinary people around you need to take that into account in their interactions with you. Your work as a trial lawyer entitles you to ask more of the people around you than you otherwise could.

Actually, no. Sorry. This trial lawyer thing is your journey, not theirs. *You* signed up for it; they didn't. As friends or family members, they have the right to an implicit understanding with you: they will love you and support your journey, and you will love them and support their journeys.

You may perceive your journey as more important or more difficult than theirs. Even assuming you are right—a dangerous assumption—you can demand more of yourself, but not more of them. Being a trial lawyer is not a license to be detached, irritable, preoccupied, or too busy for the people closest to you.

Like anyone, you will be that way at times. Like any trial lawyer, you will struggle with the difficulty of simultaneously being the best lawyer, partner, parent, spouse, and friend that you can be. You will inevitably fall short at times. That is excusable. What is *not* excusable is an attitude of being *entitled* to fall short. Many good people have fallen into this trap. It has destroyed relationships, families, and careers. Beware.

## The Trap of Excessive Guilt

You miss your daughter's softball game or your son's science fair. You are away on a deposition on your wedding anniversary. If you are a trial lawyer, despite your best efforts, absences like this are going to happen with some frequency.

You compare your parenting with that of the fathers and mothers in the television shows and Disney movies you watched growing up. Or you compare your parenting to what you imagine the conscientious parents you see at school functions are doing. You are obviously falling short. Your poor spouse is stuck picking up the slack. Everyone in your family suffers for your career choice. You enjoy your job, and they suffer. How can you not feel guilt? This guilt can sap your personal and professional life of joy and energy.

Notice that much of this guilt comes from comparing yourself to an ideal parent or an ideal spouse. (You might want to reread Chapter Nine about perfection.) Whenever we compare ourselves to some sort of ideal, we always come up short. This is true whether we are talking about trial performance or parenting.

Instead, why don't you compare yourself to the Navy officer who is away from home for three to six months at a time? To the innumerable people who work evening or night shifts to support their families? Are they bad parents too? What exactly does it mean to be a "good" parent?

Think about what you *are* providing your family. It's likely you provide them with a decent standard of living—or will soon. We often take this for granted in this country, but it's still a big deal.

You are showing them, by the way you live your life, that having a job you enjoy is an important part of having a fulfilling life. You are showing them that being engaged in the larger world is invigorating and rewarding. You are showing them that helping others gives an added meaning to life that cannot be obtained in any other way.

When you share your clients' stories, your victories, and your defeats with your family, you enrich their lives. When you share your own struggles to become a better person and a better trial lawyer with them, you help them become better people. You give them someone to be proud of.

If you are lucky, you have family and friends who appreciate the gifts your job brings to them. They help to keep you grounded somewhere on the middle of the continuum. They demand attention when you get too preoccupied, they puncture your self-inflated ego when needed, and they support and love you, even when you miss the science fair.

# CHAPTER THIRTY-ONE

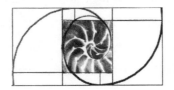

# Competitors and Comrades

In a sense, your fellow trial lawyers are competitors. They are businesspeople trying to obtain the same good cases you want. This limited truth can blind you to the larger truth that we trial lawyers need each other to survive.

Politically, we need each other. Were it not for the efforts of AAJ and the state trial lawyer associations, corporate America would have irrevocably destroyed the right to civil justice by now. Were it not for the efforts of NACDL and other forms of networking by criminal defense lawyers, the criminal justice system would be in tatters.

To win, we need each other. Through sharing information, from one trial lawyer to another, some of the most significant verdicts have been obtained. Civil defendants and prosecutors hate it when we share information. The truth may be hidden in a particular case, but our sharing of information virtually guarantees it will eventually come out.

To make money, we need each other. Many trial lawyers fail to grasp that a fellow trial lawyer's success helps us all. If the lawyer across town goes to trial in a case similar to yours and gets a significant verdict, the settlement value of your case goes up. If the lawyer across town loses a case, the settlement value of your case goes down. Similarly, if a criminal defense lawyer wins a trial, the prosecution is more likely to be reasonable in plea discussions with the next defense lawyer who comes along.

We need each other to brainstorm. No one has all the answers. When we network and brainstorm online and in person, we participate in a synergy that helps us all better serve our clients.

We need each other to joint-venture cases together. More and more often, sole practitioners and small law firms band together to handle cases. This trend is borne of necessity, as cases become more complex and expensive. Neither of us may be able to competently handle a particular case alone, but when we aggregate our knowledge, skill, and resources, we can be formidable. Plus, it is more enjoyable—or at least comforting—to have someone in the foxhole with you.

Which brings me to my last point: we need each other for emotional support. No one will ever understand your professional pain and joy like another trial lawyer. Some of the finest people you will ever meet are trial lawyers. They will give you comfort, make you laugh, and help you screw up your courage to go back to the courtroom for another day. Then, they'll buy you a drink and tell you what a brave son-of-a-bitch you were for even attempting that impossible case.

# CHAPTER THIRTY-TWO

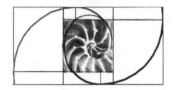

# Partners and Staff

On an hour-by-hour, day-by-day basis, nothing is more important to the emotional well-being of a trial lawyer than to have supportive partners and staff. This should be obvious, but to some trial lawyers it is not.

Simply stated, trying cases is a team sport. Trying cases involves more than a trial lawyer's time in the courtroom talking to the judge and jury. Trying cases includes the years of preparation before trial, digesting depositions, marking exhibits, conducting legal research, investigating facts, typing briefs, making travel arrangements for witnesses, and carrying boxes to the courthouse. The list could go on and on. Except in the simplest of cases, it is impossible to try a case without the help of others.

Partners and staff can be more conscientious and committed to victory than the trial lawyer—and just as essential to success. If partners and staff do a good job, they make the lawyer look good. If they make mistakes, *it is the lawyer's responsibility*. Trial lawyers need people they can trust and rely on, yet they commonly take partners and staff for granted or, worse, treat them with a dismissive attitude as a "supporting cast."

Part of your job as a trial lawyer is to take care of your team. At a minimum, that means making sure you pay them fairly and treat them with respect. Beyond that, if you have any sense, you will also *listen to them*. They understand some aspects of trying cases better than you do. They see things you miss. They have good ideas you would never think of. They are an important resource. Becoming a real trial lawyer means learning to treat them that way.

# CHAPTER THIRTY-THREE

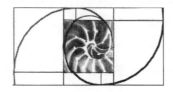

# The Key to Unhappiness

I can't tell you the key to happiness as a trial lawyer, but I do know the key to unhappiness—at least one of the most common keys. We trial lawyers have a way of tormenting ourselves.

Why does this job, which can be so challenging, exciting, and rewarding, also cause us so much unhappiness? The usual suspects—workload, financial stress, lack of civility, an adversarial system that rewards only winning—all play a part in our unhappiness. But I believe there is a more basic and far-reaching root cause of unhappiness among trial lawyers. We can find it within ourselves: our idealism. Stated more accurately, it is our *naive* idealism.

From the time we entered grade school until the time we were sworn in as lawyers, we were taught that we have the best legal system in the world. Our system presumes the accused is not guilty, the courtroom is a level playing field, the goal of the courts and judges is justice, and the judges are fair and impartial. We have a government of laws, not of men. All participants should follow the rules, and if they don't, they will be caught and punished. The list goes on and on.

Although we all began our legal careers with mixed motives and goals, most of us possessed an almost religious faith in the judicial system. We knew the system wasn't perfect, but with our help, it would get there. Even those of us just in it for the money (you know who you are) assumed we had found a corner of the free-market system where a certain order and fairness prevailed. The rules were rational and applied evenhandedly—the ultimate meritocracy.

Think of any aspect of the system, from the grand jury to the Civil Rule 26 disclosure statement. The gap between how it is supposed to work and how it actually works is often vast. Why is this so? I could advance many reasons, I suppose. The ones trial lawyers cite most often can be expressed by simply picking any word from Column A to go with any word in Column B:

| COLUMN A | COLUMN B |
|---|---|
| *Stupid* | *Judge* |
| *Lazy* | *Opposing Counsel* |
| *Dishonest* | *Witness* |
| *Biased* | *Jurors* |
| *Incompetent* | *Client* |

How we react—internally and externally—to the gap between the myth of the judicial system and the reality is at the core of much of our unhappiness. Let's look at some of the more common coping strategies. All of us have engaged in each of them to one degree or another. Usually, we engage in more than one at a time.

## Keeping Score of the System's Shortcomings

We don't just note when the system fails, we lovingly keep score. "This is the third time the judge has overruled my valid objections." "Your honor, this is the fifth time defense counsel has failed to respond to valid discovery requests."

We raise our grievances to anyone who will listen: judges, co-counsel, opposing counsel, law partners, spouses, and friends. We return from court triumphant. "Guess what the judge did today?" We have our "victory" with each shortcoming exposed. Surely, now that opposing counsel has been exposed and embarrassed, this outrageous conduct will cease. Surely *now* the judge will act.

Maybe we tell ourselves we are trying to expose these problems and fix the system. Maybe what we are really doing is trying to calm our own anxiety over the gap between how the system should work and how it actually works. Either way, we are in danger of losing track of our prime objective—winning the case.

## Becoming a Victim

"It's so unfair, isn't it? The judges are against me, our opponents don't follow the rules, and the jurors are stupid. Everything just goes to prove that I am unfairly suffering. I want everyone to know that. I will keep looking for evidence that my clients and I are being mistreated and cheated. As my search continues, I may actually lose sight of the fact that there is a way to win the case. Of course, if I am the victim of mistreatment, no one can blame me for losing, can they?"

## Becoming a Zealot

"It is unfair, damn it, and I'm not going to stand for it! There are the evildoers, and there is me. They are going to get what's coming to them. Anything I do is justified, because this is a battle between good and evil. I will fight them, I will expose them, and I will make them pay at all costs—even if I must lose the case in the process."

## Becoming Cynical and Bitter

"The whole process is corrupt. It's just a game. I can play it too. I'm through getting excited about it. I'll just look out for number one. That's what everyone else does. Since the whole thing is a game, it doesn't really matter if I win or lose."

## A New Perspective

Paradoxically, the very idealism that brought us to our vocation can corrode our ability to pursue it effectively. And it can make us very unhappy. The thoughts and feelings described above lead to unhappiness. In fact, they can cause us to wallow in our unhappiness.

I would like to propose a new way of thinking about the gap between our ideal system and the one we work in. Consider this: *If the system were fair, we'd hardly be needed.* With fair, impartial judges, scrupulously honest opponents, and intelligent, perceptive jurors, how much would a client need us?

Our clients hire us to enter an unfair system and extract some justice from it. *For us to complain about unfairness is like firefighters complaining there is too much smoke for them to put out the fire.*

Let's take federal court, for example. In many parts of the country, the federal court system has a well-deserved reputation as a place where plaintiff cases and criminal defenses go to die. Imagine a client coming to your office and having the following conversation:

*You:* We can file in state court, but there is a chance the case will be removed to federal court.

*Client:* What does that mean?

*You:* The judges usually do everything they can to help corporate and government defendants. Your chances of getting fair treatment are slim. I'm afraid if the case is removed to federal court, I won't be able to represent you. I don't like going over there; it is just so unfair.

*Client:* Can you tell me where I could find a real lawyer?

Let me say it again: *Our clients hire us to enter an unfair system and extract some justice from it.* If that is our job, nobody wants to hear us complain about it—not our partners, not our spouses, and especially not our clients.

I am not saying we shouldn't try to improve the system any way we can. I am not saying we can't tell war stories about unfair treatment at the hands of difficult judges. I am not saying we shouldn't tell our clients what they are up against. But there is a difference between complaining and problem solving, between reveling in your unfair treatment and letting off steam with war stories. We all know the difference when we watch and listen to other lawyers. In the end, it is a question of self-discipline.

Let me give you an example. We have all been in front of what I call the hundred-to-one judge. This is the judge that believes it is better for a hundred plaintiffs to be undercompensated than for even one to be overcompensated. Chances are, the judge holds this belief sincerely and probably subconsciously. This belief colors every ruling.

The criminal equivalent is the judge who believes his job is to see that defendants are convicted in an expeditious and orderly way. Again, the judge likely holds this belief sincerely and probably subconsciously. This belief colors every ruling.

Our job is not to change these judges' core values; we can't do that. Our job is not to expose their stupidity; they are probably not stupid. Our job is not to expose their unfairness; they are probably very fair people—given the emotional and intellectual framework in which they operate. Our job is to get them to see that what we are asking for is just and right—given *their* view of the world. Or maybe to show them that they have little or no choice—given the law—to do other than what we ask. Either way, we must enter the burning building. This takes technical skill, courage, and self-discipline, but we can do it. We will not always be successful, but we will have more success than if we employ the coping strategies outlined above.

Sometimes, the smoke is thick, and the flames are so hot you can feel them from across the street. The building starts to crumble before your eyes. Can you go in and get out with some justice for your client? Sometimes the answer is no. But chances are, not many lawyers are elbowing you aside to rush into that burning building ahead of you.

If we think of ourselves as firefighters entering the burning building, we might discover several things. First, we might discover that the smoke is not as thick (the system not so unfair) as we believed. Self-pity, cynicism, and zealotry have a way of distorting our perceptions. With the detachment of the firefighter, we may see more clearly.

Second, we can reclaim our idealism—a more mature idealism. It is our sweat, our tears, and whatever comes dripping out of our souls when we are in that fire that lubricates this system. It is our job to enter the burning building. And that is something to be very proud of.

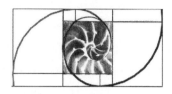

# Afterword

Everything you experience in life is an opportunity to improve your ability as a trial lawyer. Experiences as mundane as standing in a grocery checkout line or as profound as a death in the family are challenges to confront the difficulties of the human condition. As a trial lawyer, you must do more than cope; you must struggle to understand. In the end, understanding is your most powerful weapon.

You must struggle to understand yourself. You must struggle to understand others, whether they are judges, clients, witnesses, jurors, or opponents. You must struggle to understand psychology, philosophy, medicine, engineering, and arcane fields of human knowledge most people will never hear of.

As you struggle to understand, you will discover things about yourself that will surprise you—some pleasant, some unpleasant. All these discoveries will help you become a better trial lawyer, if that is where your road is meant to take you.

Your struggle for understanding may at first appear to be nothing more than a professional journey. Every experience, every bit of knowledge arms you further for the trials to come. But as the years pass, the struggle for understanding transcends trial practice; you will find personal truths more valuable than your best verdicts.

# Recommended Reading List

Any recommended list of trial advocacy books is outdated as soon as it is written. New good stuff is coming out all the time. Old good stuff is going out of print all the time. Here are the books I would recommend to anyone determined to become a good trial lawyer. These are a starting point.

If I had it to do over again, here is the order in which I would read them:

*Cross-Examination: Science and Techniques,* by Larry S. Pozner and Roger J. Dodd (Michie, 1993). This is the definitive book on cross-examination. Any trial lawyer who has not read this book should be ashamed. Learn their techniques. When you have mastered them, do not be afraid to cast them aside when the occasion warrants it.

*Recovering for Psychological Injuries,* by William A. Barton (2d ed., ATLA Press, 1990). Don't let the title fool you. Great trial wisdom and insight jump off almost every page of this book, insight and wisdom applicable to any plaintiff's case. Trial Guides plans a third edition of this book in 2009.

*Winning Jury Trials: Trial Tactics and Sponsorship Strategy,* by Robert Klonoff and Paul Colby (3rd ed., NITA, 2007). This is one of the best trial strategy and tactics book written in the last twenty years. The authors have articulated ways of thinking about jury trials that talented and experienced trial lawyers have instinctively followed for years. They explain better than anyone how to think about presenting a case.

*Rules of the Road: A Plaintiff Lawyer's Guide to Proving Liability,* by Rick Friedman and Patrick Malone (Trial Guides, 2006). Okay, Pat and I wrote this book and it feels odd to be recommending my own book. But we wrote it because there wasn't another one out there that address head-on the three major enemies of a plaintiff's case: complexity, confusion, and ambiguity. This book is full of our best ideas for making a plaintiff's liability case powerful and clear.

Anything by Gerry Spence, but especially *Win Your Case* (St. Martin's Press, 2005), which contains the most practical advice of any of Spence's books.

*David Ball on Damages: The Essential Update,* by David Ball (rev. ed., NITA, 2005). There is a reason this is the most talked-about trial advocacy book in the last thirty years. Read the book and find out.

*Polarizing the Case: Exposing and Defeating the Malingering Myth,* by Rick Friedman (Trial Guides, 2007). The most common— almost universal—civil defense is that the plaintiff is exaggerating or faking injuries. The most common questions I get when I teach are how to deal with the variants of this defense. This book contains my best answers to those questions.

*Moe Levine on Advocacy,* by Moe Levine (Trial Guides, 2008). Moe Levine was recognized in his lifetime as one of the greatest personal injury lawyers who ever lived. This book includes his closing arguments as well as writings on medical malpractice. If you want to watch Moe in action, watch the ATLA video from the Masterworks Series, entitled *Comparative Closing Arguments on Damages,* featuring Marvin E. Lewis and Moe Levine (ATLA Video, 1993). It will give you chills.

*Opening Statements,* by Al Julien (Callaghan, 1980). There is no better book for teaching you how to do an opening statement. Read it carefully; it is like sitting at the feet of a master.

*Who Will Speak for the Victim? A Practical Treatise on Plaintiff's Jury Argument,* by Jim M. Perdue (State Bar of Texas, 1989). This is a true encyclopedia of plaintiff's arguments for all situations. I have returned to this book again and again on the eve of closing argument, looking for and finding inspiration.

When you have read these books, you are ready to start exploring on your own. Have fun. Scores of exciting books are out there, more books on trial advocacy techniques, biographies, autobiographies, and accounts of individual cases. When you find a good one, please get back to me, and let me know. The search for inspiration never ends.